SACAGAWEA'S SON

The Life of Jean Baptiste Charbonneau

MARION TINLING

Mountain Press Publishing Company
Missoula, Montana

Library of Congress Cataloging-in-Publication Data

Tinling, Marion, 1904–
    Sacagawea's son: the life of Jean Baptiste Charbonneau /
Marion Tinling.
        p. cm.
    Includes bibliographical references (p.) and index.
    ISBN 0-87842-432-6 (alk. paper)
        1. Charbonneau, Jean-Baptiste, 1805-1885. 2. Sacagawea,
    1786-1884—Family. 3. Lewis and Clark Expedition (1804-
    1806)—Biography. 4. Pioneers—West (U.S.)—Biography.
    5. Shoshoni Indians—Biography. 6. Trappers—West (U.S.)—
    Biography. 7. Frontier and pioneer life—West (U.S.) I. Title.

F592.7C43 T55 2001
978'.02'092—dc21
[B]   2001032609

PRINTED IN THE UNITED STATES

Mountain Press Publishing Company
P.O. Box 2399 • Missoula, MT 59806
406-728-1900 • 800-234-5308

To Jaime, Nora, and Nicholas

CONTENTS

ACKNOWLEDGMENTS

A host of friends and correspondents have given me assistance and support in researching and writing the biography of Jean Baptiste Charbonneau. I am indebted to Enid L. Pike, certified graphologist, for a perceptive analysis of Charbonneau's handwriting. My thanks also go to the archivist of the Santa Barbara Mission for allowing access to records of the San Luis Rey Mission. Bud Gardner, writing coach, taught me perseverance; fellow writers Cleo Kocol and Mary Lucille Johnson spent much time helping to liven up the rhetoric. Others were good enough to read the manuscript in various stages: the late Professor Irving W. Anderson, authority on the Charbonneau family, kept me on the historical trail; Persia Woolley, Terri Dodge, and the late Ruth Colter-Frick, descendant and biographer of John Colter, also read the manuscript. Eleanor Fait and Ruth Ward continued to be interested in the progress of the work and made valuable suggestions. Robin Williams, producer of the video "The Trail: Lewis & Clark Expedition, 1803–1806," gave me good advice. My friends Lucille Hood and Lois Revak drove all the way from Sacramento to Charbonneau's gravesite to take photos. Above all, I am thankful for the knowledgeable and careful editing by Gwen McKenna of Mountain Press.

A Note on Spelling and Pronunciation

In the early 1800s most writers spelled words as they heard them. "Charbonneau" had many variations: Sharbono, Shavono, Charbono, etc. Lewis and Clark usually spelled "Sacagawea" as four or five syllables with spaces or dashes between them. Modern writers also spell her name in several different ways.

In quotations from Lewis and Clark I have used their original spelling. In quotations from other writers I have modernized the spelling and punctuation, except for proper names.

The following are acceptable pronunciations:

Jean: zhon

Baptiste: Bap-TEEST

Charbonneau: SHAR-bun-NO

Sacagawea: SAC-a-ja-WE-a *or* sa-CA-ga-WE-uh

rendezvous: ron-day-VOO

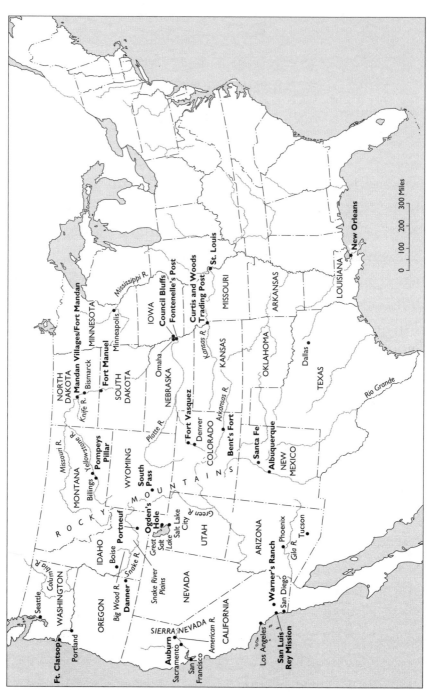

Important places in Jean Baptiste Charbonneau's life —Map by William L. Nelson

INTRODUCTION

JEAN BAPTISTE CHARBONNEAU was born to a young Shoshoni woman, Sacagawea, and French Canadian fur trapper Toussaint Charbonneau at a Hidatsa village in the winter of 1805. As an infant, Baptiste accompanied his parents on the famous journey of Lewis and Clark's Corps of Discovery, for which both his father and his mother served as guides and interpreters. Sacagawea was the only woman and the only full-blood Indian on that historic voyage, and little Baptiste was the youngest member of a major expedition in history. Eventually, most of the men in the Corps of Discovery were all but forgotten. Although Sacagawea remained widely recognized for the courageous woman she was, her son faded into near anonymity.

Two hundred years later, Americans have a renewed interest in the Corps of Discovery's momentous contribution to our nation. Historians have established historical markers and interpretive centers along the Lewis and Clark Trail to guide and inform visitors. Books, articles, and television productions are helping to make the story popular. Sacagawea and her babe have been honored on a United States coin.

By now, the stories of Meriwether Lewis and William Clark and the particulars of their journey have been told so often and so well that this book does not attempt to add to the list. Sacagawea became an icon of American history, and many books have been written about her life as well. It is her son, Jean Baptiste Charbonneau, or "Pomp," whom we will discuss here.

This Leonard Crunelle statue of Sacagawea with baby Pomp is one of many artistic tributes to the mother and child. This one stands in Bismarck, North Dakota. —Courtesy State Historical Society of North Dakota

As an infant, Baptiste charmed William Clark, who later paid for the boy's education in St. Louis. As a young man, he impressed the traveling Duke of Württemberg, who took him to Europe as his companion for six years. Upon his return to America, Baptiste went west to work in turn as a trapper, hunter, guide, and gold miner. Highly skilled as both frontiersman and scholar, he could communicate in English, French, Spanish, German, and several Indian languages. He was known as a dependable, likable, and well-informed man.

A witness to and participant in many events of western development, Jean Baptiste Charbonneau was a figure of true historical significance. His life story reveals more than the biography of a man, it represents the greater story of American western expansion. Baptiste was born at the beginning of America's dream of possessing the West, and he died just after the dream had come true, when the United States finally reached from coast to coast. In between, he played an active part in the transformation of the West, thus continuing the journey that began with Lewis and Clark.

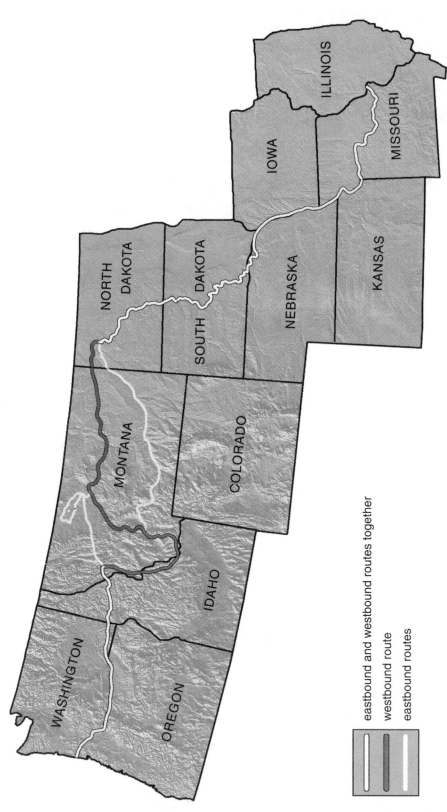

The Corps of Discovery's route to the Pacific and back —Courtesy North Dakota Tourism and National Park Service

eastbound and westbound routes together

westbound route

eastbound routes

ONE

BORN TO TRAVEL

1805 TO 1806

On the evening of February 11, 1805, Captain Meriwether Lewis recorded an event he thought worthy of including in a report to the president of the United States. He wrote:

About five o'clock this evening one of the wives of Charbono was delivered of a fine boy. It is worthy of remark that this was the first child which this woman had borne, and as is common in such cases, her labor was tedious and the pain violent. Mr. Jessaume [an interpreter] informed me that he frequently administered a small portion of the rattle of the rattlesnake, which he assured me had never failed to produce the desired effect, that of hastening the birth of the child. Having the rattle of a snake by me, I gave it to him and he administered two rings of it to the woman, broken in small pieces with the fingers and added to a small quantity of water. Whether this medicine was truly the cause or not I shall not undertake to determine, but I was informed that she had not taken it more than ten minutes before she brought forth.

The baby's father, a French Canadian fur trapper, named him Jean Baptiste.

Lewis and William Clark were co-captains of a crew of thirty-four soldiers and hired men known as the Corps of Discovery. The men were staying near the homes of the Mandan and Hidatsa Indians, on the Knife River where it joined the upper Missouri River, in what is now North Dakota. They were spending the winter there, waiting for warmer weather so they could release their boats from the inches-thick ice and resume the journey they had begun many months before.

The corps was on an expedition to explore the American West from the Missouri to the Pacific coast, looking to expand trade routes. President Thomas Jefferson had authorized the expedition and appointed Lewis and Clark to carry it out. The United States had just purchased from France the Louisiana Territory, a piece of land that more than doubled the size of the nation. The Louisiana Territory encompassed the country west of the Missouri River north to Canada, westward across the Rocky Mountains to the British possessions on the Pacific coast, and south to the lands claimed by Mexico. This turn of events gave the corps' mission even more urgency, as the president was eager to find out what the new territory was like.

If the corps succeeded in their mission, they would be the first white people to cross this territory—the land was unexplored and unmapped. It was believed that no one lived between the upper Missouri and the Pacific coast, except perhaps "uncivilized savages." The captains hoped to find the so-called Northwest Passage through the mountains and a river route that would take them all the way to the Pacific. They would eventually discover that neither the passage nor the river route existed. Yet their historic journey would open the doors to a whole new world for the American people. The Corps of Discovery expedition set out from their camp near St. Louis on May 14, 1804.

In October 1804, on their way up the Missouri, the corps was lucky to find the friendly Mandan and Hidatsa, whose villages were the northernmost settlements in the western territory. The Mandan were a fun-loving people who lived in permanent earthen lodges, grew grains and vegetables on the plains, and lived more or less at peace with their neighbors. About four thousand people lived in the prosperous villages, which served as trading posts where nomadic Indians brought furs in exchange for goods carried by American and Canadian traders.

Upon reaching the villages, Lewis and Clark offered their hands in friendship to the Mandan and Hidatsa. They gave the Indians gifts and smoked the pipe of peace with the chiefs. The tribes allowed the corps to stay and showed their guests great hospitality.

Knowing they would need shelter from the frigid northern winter, the corps built a log fort near the villages and called it Fort Mandan. The Indians were fascinated by the fort and its inhabitants, visiting frequently. They were amazed at the mountains of supplies and goods the white men had brought in their boats: guns, medicines, fabrics, scientific instruments, metal tools and knives, glass beads, mirrors, bells, and many other items the Indians had seldom, perhaps never, seen.

The expedition members asked the Mandan for information about the territory they were going to explore. The Indians were happy to assist them, scratching on the ground with sticks maps of as much of the land as they knew. The corps also asked passing traders for any information they had. The captains gained enough knowledge to plot out a surprisingly accurate map for the next part of their journey.

Toussaint Charbonneau, who had lived for some years with the Hidatsa, spoke several Indian tongues and was an experienced frontiersman. The captains hired him as an interpreter for the Indians they might meet on their travels. Toussaint wished to take the younger of his two wives with him—Sacagawea, about sixteen years old.

A Shoshoni (or Snake) from the far west (in what is now Idaho), Sacagawea was captured when she was about twelve by raiding Hidatsa, longtime enemies of the Shoshoni. She had been on a hunt with a band of her people when the Hidatsa warriors attacked. Sacagawea tried to run, but she couldn't get away. Her kidnappers brought her back to their villages as a slave. Slavery was common among Indians as well as in much of white society up to the mid-nineteenth century. Eventually Sacagawea was sold to Toussaint and became his wife. In many cultures in those days, a female slave and a wife were often the same thing.

Lewis and Clark agreed to take Sacagawea along as "interpretess" for the expedition. That winter Toussaint and Sacagawea, who was expecting a child, moved into Fort Mandan. It was here that Jean Baptiste Charbonneau was born.

Why did the captains decide to take on this rigorous and dangerous mission a young woman with a little baby? They had been reluctant at first. Then they found out that Sacagawea came from the far west and could still understand the Shoshoni language. This was important because the Shoshoni were said to have great herds of horses, which the captains had learned the corps was going to need. The Mandan had told them that there would be places where they would need to carry their boats and all their baggage overland, and they would need horses to do that. Someone who could speak the Shoshoni language might be a great help in obtaining them.

Charles M. Russell's Lewis and Clark on the Lower Columbia *shows Sacagawea, with young Pomp in a cradleboard on her back, signing to the Chinook Indians.* —Courtesy Amon Carter Museum

Moreover, Sacagawea knew a good part of the country they would be traveling over and could act as a guide.

After the ice broke in the river, in April 1805, the explorers pushed off for their journey into the unknown. Lewis wrote, "We are now about to penetrate a country at least two thousand miles in width, on which the foot of civillized man had never trodden; the good or evil it had in store for us was for experiment yet to determine."

Sacagawea wrapped her two-month-old infant in soft skins and placed him in a sling over her shoulder. As she stepped into one of the boats, little Baptiste became, as one scholar wrote, "the most unlikely member of a major geographical expedition."

Baptiste was too young to remember the great trek. But his growing mind absorbed the sights, sounds, and smells around him. He suffered along with his mother and the men all the difficulties of the long journey—cold, heat, and dampness; gnats, fleas, and mosquitoes, which bit him so badly that his face became "much puffed up & Swelled," according to Clark's journal. Later the boy learned much about the experience from stories his parents told him.

Though the corps did not find the routes they were looking for, they did find amazingly beautiful country. In their journals Lewis and Clark told the full tale of how they followed the Missouri's course through plains filled with buffalo and other wildlife, crossed the massive Rocky Mountains (which were much higher and greater in expanse than anyone had expected), and reached the mighty western rivers that pounded their way through canyons toward the Pacific Ocean. They wrote of plants and animals new to science, adding careful drawings and precise measurements. They also wrote of meeting many natives who lived in the far reaches of the country. The captains described the tribes' customs and appearance and told of their kindness to the white strangers. Their reports would dispel many false ideas Americans had about the West and its people.

Sacagawea and her child were valuable members of the expedition and contributed to its success in many ways. The presence of a woman and a child protected the travelers by showing that they came in peace and were not a threat. Sacagawea not only translated and guided but gathered wild edible plants to help feed the men. She also saved Lewis and Clark's priceless journals from washing away in a storm one day. For her critical role in the expedition, Sacagawea remains one of America's best-loved historical heroines.

While Sacagawea won the respect of the captains for her fortitude and courage, little Baptiste won their affection. His exuberance amused and cheered the men. William Clark, who was particularly fond of Baptiste, nicknamed him Pomp, also Pompey, and called him "my little dancing boy."

How did Captain Clark choose the name Pomp for little Baptiste? It is a mystery, and as with most mysteries there have been several guesses at the answer. The one accepted by most historians is that Clark heard Sacagawea call her son by that name, a Shoshoni word meaning "leader" that was often used as a nickname for a Shoshoni family's firstborn son. It is also possible that Clark, in fun, called the boy after the Roman general Pompey. It could also have been a humorous reference to the English word "pomp," meaning a gaudy display, perhaps in response to the antics of the "little dancing boy."

In August 1805, several months after leaving the Mandan villages, the explorers met the Shoshoni and bought horses from them. Amazingly, they found the very band to which Sacagawea belonged, and more amazingly, her brother was its chief! Sacagawea was overjoyed at the reunion.

The expedition reached the Pacific coast in November 1805. After spending the winter there, they departed for home in

Pompeys Pillar, near Billings, Montana
—Photo by Bill and Jan Moeller

March 1806. On the way back, Pomp became sick with a fever and swelling around his neck, perhaps mumps. The captains applied a salve of pine resin, beeswax, and bear fat on his neck, covered with a poultice of wild onions. The child recovered in about two weeks.

During the return voyage, on the Yellowstone River, the corps spotted an enormous rock cliff near present Billings, Montana. The two-hundred-foot sandstone formation had been marked with Indian paintings and carvings, called petroglyphs. Clark climbed the rock to leave his own mark there, carving "Wm Clark July 25 1806". The captain named the rock Pompey's Tower, after little Baptiste. It is known today as Pompeys Pillar.

In mid-August 1806 the boats arrived back at the Mandan villages, where the Charbonneau family would soon bid goodbye to the Corps of Discovery. Pomp was now eighteen months old. He and his parents had been part of one of the great historic journeys of all time.

TWO

INDIAN BOY

1806 TO 1809

 At the Mandan villages, Captain Clark paid Toussaint for his services. In his journal notes of August 17, 1806, Clark mentioned an intriguing offer he made to the young father:

> Took our leave of T. Chabono, his Snake Indian wife and their child who had accompanied us on our rout to the pacific ocean in the capacity of interpreter and interpretes. . . . I offered to take his little son a butifull promising child who is 19 months old to which they both himself & wife wer willing provided the child had been weened. they observed that in one year the boy would be sufficiently old to leave his mother & he would then take him to me if I would be so freindly as to raise the child for him in such a manner as I thought proper, to which I agreed.

The next day, Clark, Lewis, and most of the rest of the corps continued downriver toward St. Louis and their homes. One of the explorers, John Colter, decided instead to accompany some fur trappers heading back to the wilderness, where more adventure awaited him. In St. Louis, the people rejoiced at the return of the corps, for the men had been gone over two years, and many people assumed they had perished. After

15

celebrating in town, the men went their separate ways, back to their homes and families. Captains Lewis and Clark went on to Washington to report the findings of their journey to President Jefferson.

At the villages, the Charbonneau family soon returned to normal life with the Hidatsa. From his home on the Knife River, Baptiste could see the cottonwood trees bordering the river and, beyond that, the low hills of the western prairies, covered with short grass that rippled in the wind.

While most plains tribes lived in tepees and traveled from place to place following the buffalo, the Hidatsa and Mandan were exceptions. They had permanent settlements and planted crops. Families lived in dome-shaped earth lodges, placed close together. A large central area was used for festivals and ceremonies that included stories, songs, dances, and religious rituals. Around the villages the tribe built large palisades as protection from enemy attacks.

The lodges were built partly underground and made of a strong framework of timbers covered with earth. The roofs of willow branches, grass, and earth were a foot or more thick, so strong that the people could walk and sit on them. A large hole in the middle of the roof let light in and allowed smoke to escape from the fire pit below.

Each lodge was large enough to house a big family and all their possessions, including their dogs and even their best horses! In cold or rainy weather, the lodge's only entrance would be covered with animal skins. Lining the walls were comfortable beds, made of hides stretched over a wooden

A drawing of the Mandan villages by Charles M. Russell —Courtesy Amon Carter Museum

frame; these were curtained off with decorated hides. On the center posts hung shields, weapons, medicine bags, and feathered headdresses. There was always a fire burning in the central pit, usually with a kettle of meat stewing over it. Anyone who was hungry could come in and help himself to the food.

Several white artists visited the Mandan and Hidatsa and made numerous drawings and paintings of the villages, the earth lodges, and the people. Among them was George Catlin, who visited in the 1830s. He also kept extensive notes about his experiences. Here he described the Mandan at play: "Wild and garrulous groups of men, women, and children . . . are wending their way along [the river's] winding shores, or dashing and plunging through its blue waves, enjoying the luxury of swimming, of which both sexes seem to be passionately fond."

Hunters provided the village with meat, including buffalo, antelope, elk, and smaller animals and birds. The men also got fish from the river. The women tended the fields, cultivating corn, squash, pumpkins, and sunflowers. When the hunters brought in game, the women not only butchered and cooked the meat, they also had the hard and smelly job of cleaning the bones and hides. Bones were made into tools and utensils, and hides were fashioned into clothing and blankets. The women decorated the clothing with paint, fringes, beads, bones, and porcupine quills.

The Mandan and Hidatsa were small tribes with mighty enemies, including the Arikara and the Sioux. Strangely enough, much of their trade was with the same tribes they considered enemies. When they wished to trade, the Sioux or other tribesmen were temporarily "adopted" as relatives of the earth-lodge people and could then visit safely.

To white trappers and traders who came their way, most of them from Canada, the Mandan and Hidatsa had long been friendly and hospitable. A number of white men had, like Toussaint, lived with them and married Indian women. Baptiste was not the only boy with a white father and an Indian mother.

Had he stayed with the Hidatsa longer, Baptiste would have been taught hunting and survival techniques as well as warrior skills as he grew older. When boys were about seven years old, they began to participate in war games, training for defense in case of enemy attack. They were given small bows and arrows make of sticks, and for an hour or more every day they played at battle, coached by their fathers. Following the practice fighting there was a scalp dance. Baptiste probably watched these games and looked forward to being old enough to join in.

Baptiste's parents, however, had other plans for him. They remembered the promise Captain Clark had made to them, repeated later in a letter to Toussaint:

> *You have been a long time with me and have conducted yourself*
> *in such a manner as to gain my friendship, your woman who*
> *accompanied you that long dangerous and fatiguing rout to the*

Mandan Boys in a Sham War, *sketch by George Catlin*
—Courtesy Smithsonian Institution

Chapter Two

*Pacific Ocean and back diserved a greater reward for her atten-
tion and services on that rout than we had in our power to give
her at the Mandans.*

*As to your little Son (my boy Pomp) you well know my fond-
ness for him and my anxiety to take and raise him as my own
child. I once more tell you if you will bring your son Baptiest to
me I will educate him and treat him as my own child—I do not
forget the promis which I made to you and shall now repeet them
that you may be certain. . . . If you will bring down your Son,
your [wife] had best come along with you to take ceare of the boy
untill I get him. . . . Wishing you and your family great [suc-
cess] & with anxious expectations of Seeing my little dancing
boy Baptiest, I shall remain your Friend William Clark.*

No doubt Sacagawea wanted Baptiste to be able to read
and write, and hoped her son would grow up to be educated
and to accomplish great things. Someday he might even be
like Captain Clark himself. It was a few years, however, before
a boat was available to take the Charbonneaus to St. Louis.
The Arikara, who lived downriver from the Mandan, had attacked American fur boats on the Missouri, halting river travel
for several years.

Finally, in the summer of 1809, St. Louis fur trader Auguste
Chouteau brought a well-armed boat up the Missouri to the
Mandan villages. When Chouteau was ready to return to St.
Louis, Toussaint and Sacagawea took the opportunity to go
back with him. They dressed Baptiste, now four and a half, in
white boy's clothes and the family boarded the fur boat to
begin the long journey.

THREE

School Days

1809 to 1823

By the time the Charbonneau family reached St. Louis, it was nearly winter. The town seemed like a strange and scary place to the newcomers. Though it was not at that time the busy city we know today, it was full of life as a prominent port and shipping hub at the junction of two great rivers—the Missouri and the Mississippi. The territory had belonged first to Spain, then to France, and, since the Louisiana Purchase, to the United States. The westernmost American town, it was the center of a burgeoning fur industry in which almost all of its inhabitants were involved. Yet its population was actually smaller than that of the Mandan and Hidatsa villages.

People, horses, and wagons moved chaotically all around as Baptiste and his parents made their way through the noisy streets, looking for information about how to find Clark. Boats crowded the riverfront while goods were unloaded and piled up on the docks. The voices of Frenchmen, Indians, Americans, and Spaniards, all speaking their own languages, added to the din.

This rare engraving of St. Louis in 1817 was pictured on the back of a ten-dollar banknote from the Bank of St. Louis. —From the collection of Eric P. Newman. Print courtesy Missouri Historical Society

For Baptiste, this was a truly new experience. Until his parents prepared him to come here, he had never worn clothes. When cold or wet he had wrapped himself in a blanket or fur robe, like other Indian children. The shirt and pants he now wore were strange and uncomfortable. Feet that had never worn anything but moccasins felt cramped in the stiff shoes. He had a lot to learn.

The Charbonneaus were told that Clark was not in St. Louis; he was away on business in Washington and would not be back for many months. They also learned that the captain was now a general. After the expedition, he had been made superintendent of Indian Affairs for the Louisiana Territory. But Lewis, they were saddened to hear, was dead. He had been shot while on a journey back to Washington. Nobody knew whether he was murdered or killed himself in a moment of despair. The mystery remains unsolved to this day.

The family found a place to stay until Clark's return. In the meantime, they explored St. Louis, taking it all in. Small houses were crowded together along the narrow, dusty streets. People bustled in and out of the city's many shops and taverns. Toussaint probably enjoyed taking his family around the town. There was still much interest in the Corps of Discovery, and people would have been eager to see Sacagawea and the little boy who had been with the expedition. Sacagawea hoped the captain would remember his promise, and she wondered if he would recognize the sturdy boy at her side as the once-chubby little Pompey.

Toussaint was a Roman Catholic, and shortly after the Charbonneaus' arrival, on December 28, 1809, he had his son baptized at a log church by the Mississippi River. The church stood at the site of today's Gateway Arch. The church records, which were in French, named Auguste Chouteau and his eleven-year-old daughter, Eulalie, as godparents. Father Urbain Guillet, a Trappist monk, performed the baptism. Baptiste's date of birth was incorrectly recorded as February 11, 1804. Toussaint signed the record with an X. Sacagawea's name was not given; she is described only as "_____, savage of the Snake Nation."

When Clark returned to St. Louis on July 1, 1810, he was pleased to hear that Pomp and his parents were in town. The general had his own son now, Meriwether Lewis Clark, a few months old. The year before, Clark had married Julia Hancock, the woman for whom he had named the Judith River, in present-day Montana.

Toussaint bought a small piece of land from Clark on October 30, 1810, and tried farming. But he soon grew tired of St. Louis, and he sold his piece of property back to Clark just six months after he bought it. He and Sacagawea, homesick for their people, took a boat to Fort Manuel, a trading post on the Missouri River in what is now South Dakota, where they planned to stay for a while. Sacagawea, pregnant again, was obliged to go with her husband. But she left her son under the protection of a man she trusted, and of course she expected to see him again.

Baptiste's life in St. Louis was quite different from the one he had known in the Indian village. Clark enrolled him in a school for half-Indian boys run by the Reverend J. E. Welch, a Baptist minister, and Baptiste spent much of his time in a stuffy schoolroom instead of outdoors. The religious beliefs of his teacher and the other students were not at all like those of the Hidatsa. He had to get used to many customs of the white men.

On the other hand, he had a good deal of freedom to wander about and watch the activity around the waterfront. He explored old fortifications built when the town belonged to Spain. The circular stone towers, wood blockhouse, and large stone bastion were great attractions to him and his friends. And when tired of the town they could hunt and fish in the nearby woodlands.

Clark's plan to raise Baptiste as his own son did not work out. After his parents left, Baptiste lived in a boardinghouse, not with Clark's family. Because he was half Indian, it is likely that Clark's wife would not accept him into her household, nor would he ever be completely accepted into white society. Clark did, however, keep his promise to pay for the boy's education and provide amply for his needs until he was grown.

Clark's accounts of his expenditures for "J. B. Charbonneau, a half Indian" in 1820 provide an interesting glimpse into Baptiste's life growing up:

Portrait of William Clark in 1832, by George Catlin —Courtesy National Portrait Gallery, Smithsonian Institution

Jan. 22, 1820, to J. E. Welch, for two quarters' tuition, and firewood, and ink, $16.37 ½.

March 31, L. T. Honore, for boarding, lodging and washing from 1st January to 31st March, 1820, $45.00.

April 1, J. and G. H. Kennerly, for 1 Roman History, $1.50, one pair of shoes, $2.25, two pairs of socks, $1.50, one Scott's lessons, $1.50, one dictionary, $1.50, one hat, $4.00, four yards of cloth, $10.00, one ciphering book, $1.00, one slate and pencils, 62 cents.

Eventually Clark and his wife had three more sons and one daughter. In addition to Meriwether, there were William, George, John, and Mary. After Julia died in 1820 and little Mary the following year, Clark married Julia's cousin, Harriet Kennerly Radford, a widow. This added to the Clark household three stepchildren, John, William, and Mary Radford. Clark and his second wife had two more sons, Jefferson and Edmund. Edmund died as an infant and later John Clark also died, at age thirteen.

Although Baptiste knew the Clark children, they were not close. As they grew up, he and the Clarks lived in different worlds. But in the future, oddly enough, he was to cross paths with some of them in places far from St. Louis.

In 1813, when Baptiste was eight years old, his young life became clouded with tragedy. News came from the clerk at Fort Manuel, John Luttig, that Sacagawea had died of a fever at the fort on December 20, 1812, leaving an infant daughter, Lisette. Furthermore, Toussaint, who had not returned from a fur-trapping expedition farther west, was presumed dead.

Luttig brought the baby with him to St. Louis. Believing that she and Baptiste were orphans, he signed papers making himself their guardian. Later Clark went to court and assumed legal guardianship of Lisette and Baptiste. It was later discovered that Toussaint was still alive, but he was far away in the north. It is not known what became of the baby girl, but she may have died in infancy, as there are no records of her beyond that.

It must have been difficult for young Baptiste, having no parents and being removed from his native culture. Clark was away when Baptiste received the news of his mother's death. The general had taken his wife and child to Virginia for safety during the War of 1812, and he was kept busy with military affairs for the duration of the war. Even when he was in town, Clark was busy with government duties and his own family, and he no doubt had little time for his protégé.

Baptiste saw even less of his father. Toussaint was in St. Louis for a short time in 1816, when Baptiste was eleven, but his new job as a guide and interpreter for the Indian Service kept him on the road. He held that job for the next twenty-three years, serving travelers, military men, artists, scientists, and others interested in the trade, the wildlife, and the native peoples of the West.

When Baptiste first came to St. Louis, he already spoke Hidatsa and Mandan (very similar languages) and had learned some French from his father. He had also, having heard English as a baby, picked up some of that language from American traders passing through the villages. In St. Louis, people spoke English, French, Spanish, and other languages, and of course school was taught in English. Baptiste seemed to have a natural gift for languages that helped him to sort out these various tongues. He would find it a useful skill throughout his life.

In spite of great public interest in the Lewis and Clark expedition, Clark was unable to get his and Lewis's full journals published for many years after the explorers returned home. An account by Patrick Gass, a member of the Corps of Discovery, was published in 1807, and in 1814 a book based on Clark's journal was finally published as *History of the Expedition under the Command of Captains Lewis and Clark.* If Baptiste was lucky enough to acquire a copy of one of these books, he would for the first time have read the story of the epic journey in which he had taken part. Up to that time, his own undoubtedly faint memories and the stories his parents told him were all that he knew of the expedition. Now he could begin to understand and perhaps feel some pride in his parents' role in the great, historic adventure.

In 1817 General Clark built a museum next to his new home. The great room, one hundred feet long and thirty-five wide, was lit by large chandeliers and filled with items Clark had collected over the years, most of them gifts from native people. Clark also used the museum as a council chamber where he met with Indian visitors. Baptiste may have gone there to gaze on the canoes, arms, beds, clothes, ornaments, pipes, musical instruments, war bonnets, and other things that reminded him of his childhood.

But Baptiste's pride in his Indian roots may have been mixed with uncertainty. As he grew older and mingled with the towns-people, undoubtedly he was the target of prejudice and suffered from being called a "half-breed" (an often derogatory term for someone whose heritage was half white, half Indian). Many white people in those days looked upon Indians as savages and thought half-breeds had the worst qualities of both their ancestries. Shopkeepers regarded him with suspicion, assuming from his dark complexion that he could be a thief. Many white boys did not accept him as an equal. Though Baptiste did not quite fit into the world of white men, he had no tribal connection either, especially after Sacagawea's death. In many places, including the society to which General Clark and his family belonged, he was an outsider.

When Baptiste was ready to leave school, sometime between 1820 and 1823, he had to decide what he was going to do with his life. What career was open to an educated half-Indian in St. Louis? He might be a clerk for a fur company, but that job had limited potential. Joining his father as a guide and interpreter was more appealing, chiefly because it would allow him to live freely in the wilderness he loved. But soon fate stepped in and offered him a choice he could not have foreseen in his wildest dreams.

FOUR

PRINCELY YEARS

1823 TO 1829

 By June 1823 Baptiste was working at the trading post of Cyrus Curtis and Andrew Woods, located upstream from the mouth of the Kansas River (a spot in today's Kansas City, Kansas). At eighteen Baptiste had grown into a man, physically and mentally. There are no known portraits or descriptions of him, yet we know he was striking enough in appearance and personality to impress a foreign prince who was visiting the post, Paul Wilhelm, Duke of Württemberg, Germany. The prince had stopped at the Curtis and Woods camp on his way west. His interpreter and guide for the journey was Toussaint Charbonneau, Baptiste's father.

Duke Paul was traveling in the United States studying the plants and animals of the West. First arriving in New Orleans, he then went to St. Louis, where he met the merchant fur traders Pierre Chouteau and his brother Auguste. He talked to them about the upper Missouri River region, an area in which he was interested, and they showed him the reports their agents had written of conditions there. While in town Duke Paul was also pleased to meet General William Clark, who provided more information about the upper Missouri. The Chouteau brothers arranged for the prince to travel up the river in a fur company steamboat. And General Clark may have recommended a certain guide.

Though a well-educated man of high position, Duke Paul was a true explorer, and he quickly adapted to the rough conditions of the frontier. He stayed in the leaky cabins of poor settlers and ate the local fare of sour milk and cold cornbread. He was a crack shot when hunting, and he relished roasted bear meat. Though primarily a naturalist, he had broad interests and was fascinated with the native peoples of the West and their cultures.

*Chalk drawing of
Duke Paul Wilhelm
of Württemberg*
—Courtesy
Deutschordensmuseum,
Bad Mergenheim,
Germany

A traveling companion once described Duke Paul as "a man of an intellectuality far beyond ordinary comprehension. . . . His courage is so boundless that it often approaches downright madness itself. In spite of his early bringing up at one of the most exclusive royal courts in Christendom, he is utterly democratic and considerate in all his dealings with others." In short, he was the kind of man Baptiste could admire.

The Curtis and Woods trading camp, according to the prince's journal, consisted of "a few persons, Creoles and half-bloods, whose occupation is trade with the Kansa Indians, some hunting, and agriculture." Duke Paul was surprised to find at this wilderness outpost an Indian who had been educated far beyond most of his peers, a young man who could speak several languages and who took pleasure in reading. The prince was further intrigued when he found out that this young man was the son of his interpreter and of Sacagawea, whose contribution to the Lewis and Clark expedition was well known.

In spite of their vastly different backgrounds, Baptiste and Duke Paul formed an immediate friendship. On an impulse, the prince invited his new friend to go back with him to his home in Germany when he finished his trip, and Baptiste eagerly accepted. Duke Paul then left to continue his travels north and was gone for several months. When he came back to the Curtis and Woods post on his way home in October, Baptiste joined him.

The two made their way by riverboat and then horseback to St. Louis, where they boarded the steamboat *Cincinnati*, bound for New Orleans. But they got only as far as St. Genevieve, where the ship struck a sandbar and sank. The passengers had just enough time to save themselves and their possessions. They returned to St. Louis and left again, this time on the steamboat *Mandan*, which arrived in New Orleans on December 19.

Baptiste had never seen a city as large as New Orleans. Duke Paul, who had been there just a year earlier, remarked on the many changes he saw. "One year is quite sufficient," he wrote, "to bring about a great alteration in such an industrious city." While waiting for a ship to Europe, the prince and Baptiste had time to explore the city, with its Old World architecture, bustling streets, and French charm. Duke Paul had acquaintances in town, and he and Baptiste spent their layover pleasantly, with good food and congenial company. Baptiste gave up his old buckskins and bought new clothes fit for a nobleman's companion.

On December 24 the pair took passage for Europe on the brig *Smyrna*, but they had to remain onboard for two weeks, waiting for the wind to change. The passengers sat drifting on the Mississippi, plagued by mosquitoes and surrounded by alligators. One day someone shot one of these great reptiles in the head and brought it, wounded but alive, on deck. According to Duke Paul, the alligator was put into a spare barrel and was still alive when they landed in France.

When the *Smyrna* finally departed, the prince felt sad as he watched America fade from his sight: "I fixed my eyes on [the coastline] until the last sign of it had vanished without a trace in the waves of the sea. An emotion-filled moment overcame me as the last bit of land was lost from sight. I had received so many manifestations of friendship in the United States, and everywhere my journey had awakened the interest of the inhabitants. The people had been most obliging." Duke Paul does not mention Baptiste, and we can only imagine how the young man felt leaving his homeland.

It was a pleasant voyage until the ship ran into a storm near Bermuda. "From now on," the prince wrote, "the sea fought us with huge waves, and the ship was tossed about so violently that the rolling action became unbearable. The waves struck with such force over board that part of the railing was shattered. Water barrels and other gear were washed into the sea and it was almost impossible to remain on deck."

On the trip Baptiste had a chance to get better acquainted with his companion. Duke Paul, only seven years older than Baptiste, was a nephew of King Friedrich of Württemberg, a small kingdom near Stüttgart, Germany. The king had seen to it that his nephew received a good education. Although he was made an officer in the king's guard at the age of nine, the prince took no interest in military life and resigned his commission. He joked that he hoped his cousins outlived him so that he would never have to succeed to the throne. He once made this flowery declaration: "In the atmosphere of a palace I would feel like a wild thing that is imprisoned in a gilded cage. The ermine, the sceptre, and the crown would be to me the emblems of a galley slave, and my heart would never cease to hunger for the vast silent places and the simple life among free unaffected children of nature."

Duke Paul had studied under a great naturalist who had aroused in him a deep interest in science, and he decided to dedicate his life to learning as much as he could about the natural world. His visit to the United States was the realization of a dream to travel throughout the Western Hemisphere observing the plants, animals, and peoples of North and South America.

Duke Paul and Baptiste reached France on February 14, 1824, and proceeded to the prince's German estate. Duke Paul was one of the wealthiest men in Europe, and as a member of his household Baptiste lived in a world of privilege far beyond anything he could have imagined. He had been transported from the raw wilderness to a stately palace, where servants waited on him and he was treated like a prince himself. He was surrounded by the best of European art, music, and literature. For the next several years he and the prince hunted in the king's great Black Forest estates, attended cultural events, and traveled through Europe and North Africa. Baptiste soon added German to the languages he spoke.

In 1827 Duke Paul married and moved into a castle on the Tauber River. He built a museum nearby for the many plant and animal specimens and other artifacts he had collected on his travels. Baptiste assisted the prince as he sorted and labeled the exhibits, and in the process he learned much useful information about the plants and wildlife of his own country.

Duke Paul also wrote a book about his travels in North America and had a few copies privately printed in 1828. Perhaps the prince's recollections brought back his desire to travel, in spite of the fact that he now had a family. In April 1829 Duke Paul and Baptiste left for Santo Domingo, in the Caribbean, and eight months later, on December 1, 1829, they arrived in St. Louis. There the two men parted company.

Duke Paul continued up the Missouri River for further study of the region. Later he went to Mexico and many other places in the New World. He died in 1860, before completing the arrangement of his papers and collections. Most of them are now lost, though some of his travel writings survive. There is no record that he and Baptiste ever met again.

As for Baptiste, he would have had a number of choices. Being so well educated, he could have pursued work in St. Louis, perhaps a post with the Bureau of Indian Affairs, of which William Clark was superintendent. Instead, he signed on with the American Fur Company as a fur trapper shortly after his return to the United States. For the next fourteen years he would live and work in the Rocky Mountain wilderness. He could not have chosen a life more different than the one he had known with Duke Paul. Perhaps he was tired of "civilized" society and wished to live closer to nature, or perhaps he sought the adventure and freedom of a mountain man, in accord with his frontier heritage. Whatever his reasons, the decision set his course for much of the rest of his life.

FIVE

GREENHORN
MOUNTAIN MAN

1830

 When Baptiste joined John Jacob Astor's American
Fur Company in the spring of 1830, he was sent out
with the company's first fur brigade from St. Louis.
Lucien Fontenelle and Andrew Drips, who had been working
in the upper Missouri fur trade for years, led the expedition.
Baptiste's section had thirty-one men, some of whom were,
like him, inexperienced trappers, or greenhorns. One of these
newcomers was an educated nineteen-year-old from New York
named Warren Angus Ferris, who kept a daily journal of his
experiences as a trapper. Later published as a book, Ferris's
journal is an excellent record of Baptiste's group's first few
months in the mountains.

Ever since Lewis and Clark brought the news that the western streams were rich in beaver, American trappers had been
moving farther west. Beaver fur, used in making felt for men's
hats, was highly prized. Until the 1820s, British and French
Canadians had dominated the fur business, bringing furs to
U.S. markets by canoe from the north. When Astor and other

American businessmen entered the fur trade, they set up agencies in St. Louis, a more easily accessible place from which to take in and distribute furs. The Americans soon grew wealthy both from trading with Indians for pelts and from hiring their own trappers. The fur trade soon became the base of the western economy.

The first American trapping expeditions, in 1822 and 1823, traveled by boat up the Missouri River, but after several brigades suffered Indian attacks the traders decided that this route was too dangerous. They began taking a trail that went overland along the Platte River instead. The route led through South Pass (in present Wyoming), a wide and easily traveled gap through the Rocky Mountains. The pass later became part of the Overland Trail used by the pioneers. It was this route that Baptiste's brigade followed.

As the expedition got under way, the men talked and got to know one another. The majority of the men in Baptiste's group were Canadians. For the most part, the trappers were rough men with little education. Many could neither read nor write. They gave different reasons for joining the brigade, but none would admit to doing it for the money. Rather, they sought adventure, or they wanted to live a rugged, healthy life, or they wished to see nature in its "savage grandeur."

Trappers often dressed in buckskins, a fringed leather tunic over a flannel shirt and fringed leather leggings. If these garments were new, their wearers were greenhorns; if they were worn and greasy, their owners were experienced. The old-timers regaled the new recruits with hair-raising tales of mountain life. According to Warren Ferris's journal, one claimed he hunted an antelope in the Wind River Mountains for a week without rest or food. Another swore he rode on the back of a grizzly bear through a village of Blackfeet Indians. As for Baptiste's own story, chances are he knew no one would believe it, so he kept it to himself.

A Trapper and His Pony *by Frederic Remington*
—Courtesy Frederic Remington Art Museum

On the road, fifteen more men joined the party. The trappers also picked up several wagons containing trade goods, which they later loaded onto mules for the rest of the journey. The fur company supplied these goods as a kind of currency for the men to trade with Indians for necessities as well as pelts. The company also provided all the men's food, transportation, equipment, and other essential items.

When the men reached Fontenelle's trading post (in present Bellevue, Nebraska), they were given tents. They rested at the post for four weeks before moving on to another post, about thirty miles north, near Council Bluffs, Iowa. Here they were organized into small groups, given rules, and assigned chores for the trip ahead. Each company had a captain who would call them together each morning and lead the caravan during the day; he would choose the stopping places for noon and night.

For many days the trappers traveled across the Great Plains, a boundless prairie with few trees. The men followed the rivers—the Missouri and the Platte and their tributaries—that cut through increasingly parched land. The trail gradually rose to six thousand feet elevation. The rock formations and mesas that rose out of the flatlands were landmarks: Chimney Rock, Scott's Bluffs, the Red Hills, Independence Rock, Pilot Butte.

Because the trappers were traveling in a large group, they did not fear Indian attacks, but they did meet several parties of Indians along the way. Some wanted to trade with them; others demanded gifts as a toll for passing over their land.

The men also saw buffalo on the plains. Warren Ferris described the herds as "a vast expanse of moving, plunging, rolling, rushing life." One herd was so large it took three days to pass their company. The men took advantage of the opportunities to get fresh meat, which was a welcome addition to the boiled salted pork and dried corn supplied by the fur company. They also used the buffalo chips (manure) for fuel when there was no wood available.

There were other American trappers in the Snake River country that year. Some, like Baptiste and his party, were engagés, hired by a fur company to trap for it exclusively; others were free trappers, who trapped for themselves and could trade with anyone they wished. Since the American Fur Company men were new to the area, they asked the more experienced trappers about the terrain, where the best streams were, and other tips. Although they were competitors, men from different fur companies often shared information and sometimes traveled together.

Baptiste's party reached the mountains in July, and in August they separated into three smaller groups to trap in different areas. Baptiste's detachment, twenty-two mounted men led by Michel Robidoux, were sent to the Snake River plains (in present-day Idaho). Here Baptiste had a harsh introduction to his new life as a mountain man. One of the trappers with Baptiste wrote a description of the party's misadventure, which Warren Ferris included in his book.

On the way to their assigned region, Baptiste's group came to a barren area covered with masses of sharp-edged black rock. The rock was hardened lava from an ancient volcano. The men attempted to ride past the rock, but they soon realized it spread over a wide area, perhaps forty or fifty miles around. Here and there on the surface of the rock were large blisters, which when detached looked like big black pots. (One of the trappers later used one of these rock pots as a frying pan!)

As the men rode on, great chasms opened up where the lava had cracked and split as it cooled. At first they thought they could jump over the crevasses on their horses, but the gaps soon became too wide to cross. Finally they could go no farther and were forced to turn back. As the summer sun beat down on the black rock, the air became increasingly hot. The men's beaverskin water pouches were soon empty, and the men and animals grew desperately thirsty.

The trappers spent the night wandering by moonlight looking for water. The next morning, with the men facing another scorching day, the detachment leader gave orders for each man to fend for himself. Some searched for water alone, others in small groups. The horses began to give out, and some of the men collapsed on the ground, begging their companions to come back with water if they found any.

At last someone fired his gun, meaning he had found water. Even the mules and horses understood the signal and moved toward the sound. One of the trappers described the men's emotions when they reached the top of a hill and looked down:

We . . . then beheld what gave us infinitely more delight than would the discovery of . . . the richest mine of gold. . . . There lay at the distance of about four miles, the loveliest prospect imagination could present to the dazzled senses—a lovely river sweeping along through graceful curves. The beauteous sight lent vigour to our withered limbs, and we pressed on, oh! how eagerly.

Water! *by Frederic Remington* —Courtesy Frederic Remington Art Museum

By sunset they had reached the edge of the Maladi River (the present Big Wood River). Men and animals plunged in and drank. The men laughed, cried, and shouted with relief, dancing and embracing one another in the water.

They spent that night and the following morning taking water back to the men and animals left behind and then escorting them to the riverside camp. They succeeded in rescuing everyone—all except Baptiste, who had wandered from the trail. His companions feared he had perished.

Baptiste had left the group to search for water and became hopelessly lost, beyond the sight and hearing of anyone. After wandering alone for another day, he finally reached the Maladi River, but his fellow trappers were already gone. After restoring his body and his spirits with the ice-cold water and caring for his horse and mule, he went in search of his party. While scanning the landscape he glimpsed an Indian camp, but not knowing whether or not the tribe was friendly, he was afraid to approach them. Resignedly, he returned to the river and refilled his water pouch, prepared his animals, and set out alone across the Snake plains toward Portneuf, where the detachment had planned to meet.

Baptiste traveled for eleven days, trying his best to avoid hostile tribes such as the Blackfeet. Afraid to use his gun for fear of attracting the attention of the Indians, he went almost without food. The skills and knowledge he had learned from his parents and Duke Paul no doubt helped him to survive. When at last he stumbled into the camp at Portneuf, exhausted and hungry, he discovered that the rest of his party had not yet arrived. The men there took care of Baptiste and his animals, and he rested there while waiting for his detachment.

A few days later Baptiste's fellow trappers reached the camp, and they were undoubtedly relieved to find him alive and well. They told him they had waited at the river and sent scouts to look for him before they gave up the search and went on. Baptiste learned that the Indian camp he had avoided was really a group of Canadian fur trappers from the Hudson's Bay Company. Had he gone into their camp, he would have found his own party and saved himself those eleven days of toil and privation.

Baptiste later heard stories of other lost trappers—some who survived and others who were never seen alive again. He would have been especially interested in the story of John Colter and John Potts because they both had been with the Corps of Discovery. In 1808 the two men were camped on the bank of the Jefferson River when a band of Blackfeet attacked them, killing Potts. Colter, however, made an escape that would become a legend told around many a campfire. The Indians robbed Colter and stripped him of his clothes. For sport, they told him to run for his life, expecting to catch him easily. Run he did, over cactus, rock, and rubble in his bare feet, outdistancing the entire band.

One warrior finally caught up with him and lifted his spear. Colter deflected the blow, grabbed the weapon, turned it around, and plunged it into the Indian's chest. Snatching up the warrior's blanket, Colter ran for a river that lay just ahead and hid himself in the brush until the Indians gave up looking for him. Alone and defenseless, with nothing but the blanket for cover, Colter walked for over a week before reaching an American fort on the Bighorn River.

The mountains were filled with tales like this, and Baptiste knew he was not the only trapper who had faced hardship and danger. In surviving his eleven-day trek, he had proven himself and earned the respect of his fellow trappers. He was no longer a greenhorn.

During his years as a trapper, Baptiste would work the streams that flow into the great rivers both east and west of the Continental Divide—the Snake, the Salmon, the Green, the Yellowstone, and many others. Living and exploring in the Rocky Mountain area (in the present states of Montana,

Colter's Race for Life *by Charles M. Russell* —Courtesy Amon Carter Museum

Wyoming, Colorado, Idaho, and Utah), he and his companions would discover hot springs, soda springs, mud pots, geysers, and other wonders of nature. As a trapper Baptiste would live on roots and berries, fish and game, and even the meat of mules, horses, and dogs. He would suffer through sweltering heat, icy winds, and miserable dampness, fending off mosquitoes, grizzly bears, wolves, rattlesnakes, and even hostile natives.

Why did mountain men like Baptiste labor, year after year, in so hazardous and difficult an occupation? Ferris offered his interpretation:

> *They rove through this savage and desolate region free as the mountain air, leading a venturous and dangerous life, governed by no laws save their own wild impulses, and bounding their desires and wishes to what their own good rifles and traps may serve them to procure. Strange, that people can find so strong and facinating a charm in this rude nomadic and hazardous mode of life, as to estrange themselves from home, country, friends and all the comforts, elegances, and privileges of civilization; but so it is, the toil, the danger, the loneliness, the deprivation of this condition of being . . . is, they think, more than compensated by the lawless freedom, and the stirring excitement, incident to their situation and pursuits. . . . A strange, wild, terrible, romantic, hard, and exciting life they lead. . . . So attached to it do they become, that few ever leave it, and they deem themselves, nay are, with all these bars against them, far happier than the indwellers of towns and cities.*

SIX

ROUGH LIVING AND RENDEZVOUS

1830 TO 1839

After their ordeal in the lava desert, Baptiste's detachment went on to spend the winter of 1830–31 at Ogden's Hole, in present-day Utah. Expedition leaders Drips and Fontenelle and the rest of the brigade were already there, along with a detachment of the Rocky Mountain Fur Company and some free trappers. That winter was especially hard. The snow was so deep and game so scarce that the men and animals were near starvation. After Indians stole seventeen horses, the company sent two men, "a Canadian and a half breed" (perhaps Baptiste), traveling on snowshoes, to a Hudson's Bay Company camp to trade beads for horses.

In February the trappers discovered a plot by some Shoshoni Indians, a tribe that appeared to be friendly, to massacre the entire camp. Fortunately, one of the Shoshoni leaders, the Horn Chief, persuaded them not to do it, thereby gaining the friendship of the trappers. Nevertheless, the white men never fully trusted the Shoshoni after that.

Mountain men did not disguise their fear and hatred of certain tribes, especially the Blackfeet and the Sioux, along with several others. Indeed, even half-Indian trappers like Baptiste approached most natives with distrust. Yet many tribes welcomed the trappers and protected them. The Flathead, for instance, were very friendly toward whites. A chief of that tribe once told Baptiste's brigade of their first encounter with white men a quarter of a century earlier—when they had met Captains Lewis and Clark and their Corps of Discovery. That meeting impressed the Flathead so favorably that they remained lifelong friends of the whites. Perhaps Baptiste heard the chief's words and remembered stories his own mother had told him of that very meeting.

In most trapping areas, the presence of hostile tribes made the trappers' job risky. Because they often worked alone or with only one or two companions, trappers were vulnerable. Many Indians were adept at stealing horses, and a man left without his horse or mule would be stranded in the wilderness. While searching the streams for signs of beaver or wading into the water to tend the traps, a trapper often had to leave his mount and his rifle on the bank, exposed to Indians. Even having a partner to stand guard did not guarantee one's safety.

Some of Baptiste's companions, as Warren Ferris reported, were killed by hostile Indians. Blackfeet killed Daniel Richards and Henry Duchern at Camas Prairie, and a man named Frasier, an Iroquois from Canada, was shot, stripped, and left in the Jefferson River. Frasier's fellow trappers dug his grave "with an axe and frying pan." To avoid trouble, trappers learned to pay attention to small details. Ferris wrote:

> *It might seem a trifling matter to note the track of footmen, the report of firearms, the appearance of strange horsemen, and the curling vapor of a far-off fire, but these are far from trivial incidents in a region of country where the most important events are indicated by such signs only. Every man carries here emphatically his life in his hand, and it is only by the most watchful precaution, grounded upon and guided by the observation of every unnatural appearance however slight, that he can hope to preserve it.*

After the long and difficult winter, early in April 1831 the trappers at Ogden's Hole heard that the snow had left the Snake River plains. They set off, only to encounter such heavy snow that the horses could no longer proceed. The men were forced to carry the horses, tied to poles and hoisted upon their shoulders, for two miles. The next day they made a path by marching, one after another, through the drifts. At last they reached the Portneuf River and emerged onto a prairie that was bare and dry. Ferris described their relief and joy: "The sensation produced by this sudden transition from one vast and deep expanse of snow which had continually surrounded us for more than five months . . . was one of most exquisite and almost rapturous pleasure."

Sometime after the summer of 1832 Baptiste left the American Fur Company and joined those who "trap by the skin"— free trappers. He teamed up with James Bridger, the most celebrated mountain man in America. Bridger was only a year older than Baptiste. Like Baptiste, Bridger had spent much of his boyhood in St. Louis, but he did not go to school. Instead he worked, running a ferry between St. Louis and Six Mile Prairie and then working as an apprentice to a blacksmith. It may have been as early as 1822 when Bridger joined a trapping expedition to the Rockies. He remained in the mountains for the next forty-seven years.

Among other things, Jim Bridger is credited with discovering the Great Salt Lake in 1824. Tasting the water and finding it salty, he thought it was the ocean. In 1830 he and four other men formed the Rocky Mountain Fur Company. In later years Bridger explored the wonders of what is now known as Yellowstone Park. After leaving the fur business he built a fort on the Green River that served travelers on the Oregon Trail.

In June 1834 Baptiste attended his first rendezvous, an annual gathering of trappers, traders, and Indians. The rendezvous was one of the most interesting developments of the fur trade. The word *rendezvous* is French for "meeting." It was held every summer, beginning in 1825, as an opportunity for the traders to bring supplies to the trappers for the following season. In exchange the trappers brought the traders their year's catch of pelts, which the traders took to St. Louis to sell. The Indians, too, had pelts to trade for whiskey and various manufactured goods. The Indians also sold the trappers horses and items such as moccasins and pouches.

While the fur companies made tremendous profits from the trade, the trappers themselves made little money. The company traders sold the goods they brought to the rendezvous at double the price they had paid for them in St. Louis. For their labors, the mountain men received just enough supplies to live on and little more.

The location of the rendezvous differed from year to year, always in a valley with space for many people and plenty of grass for the horses and mules. It was through a mysterious chain of communication that the trappers and friendly Indians found out where that year's event was to be held. The Indians often brought their wives and children to the rendezvous with them. Hundreds of trappers and thousands of Indians attended the gatherings.

The rendezvous, which lasted about a week, were social as well as business occasions, marked by music, games of skill,

Rendezvous on the Green River *by Alfred J. Miller*
—Courtesy National Archives of Canada

dancing, storytelling, and revelry. After spending the year living the roughest kind of existence, the trappers needed some fun as much as they needed new gear. Since most of them had no real homes and few companions, the rendezvous were like big family reunions, cementing friendships as well as aggravating rivalries between the men.

One evening at his first rendezvous, Baptiste led a group of half-bloods and Indians in a mock war dance. Chanting, moccasins thumping, buckskin fringes flying, they put on a rousing good show. In the audience was James Marshall Anderson, a young man on his first trip to the Rockies, and in his journal he identifies Baptiste as "born of the squaw mentioned by Clark and Lewis, on their journey." Anderson talked to Baptiste and wrote that he was "an intelligent and interesting young man. He converses fluently and well in English, reading and writing and speaking with ease French and German—understanding several of the Indian dialects."

Another incident involving Baptiste at this rendezvous appeared in Anderson's journal. One night someone cut loose some horses and stole some halters. The next morning, as recriminations flew back and forth, Baptiste announced that he had seen a certain young white man prowling around during the night, and he accused the man of the crime. The youth denied the charge and threatened Baptiste with a flogging. Baptiste's reply to this insult was quick and decisive. In a flash, he pulled out his knife and plunged it into the man's shoulder. Someone separated the two and that was the end of the incident. Such fights were common at rendezvous, and no one thought the worse of Baptiste for defending his honor.

Baptiste undoubtedly went to several more rendezvous after that one and became acquainted with the many diverse characters who attended them. Among the most outstanding and memorable were Thomas Fitzpatrick, Kit Carson, and James Beckwourth. Later Baptiste would march with Fitzpatrick and Carson under Colonel Steven Watts Kearny and find himself stranded on a small island with Beckwourth.

Thomas Fitzpatrick was one of Jim Bridger's partners in the Rocky Mountain Fur Company. Unlike Bridger, Fitzpatrick had a fair education and was said to have "a gentlemanly bearing." He was born in Ireland and came to the United States as a young man. He joined the earliest fur-trapping parties to the Rockies, where he met Bridger. Because of an accident that crippled one hand, the Indians called Fitzpatrick "Broken Hand." Later, another experience turned his hair white, which won him the name "White Hair." He roamed the West as trapper, guide, and Indian agent until his death in 1854.

Christopher "Kit" Carson had entered the fur trade about the same time as Baptiste. Joining a trapping brigade in 1829, he went from St. Louis to Santa Fe and Taos, then to California. Later he partnered with Thomas Fitzpatrick and spent some years trapping in the same areas as Baptiste. The 1834 rendezvous was Carson's first, too.

In 1842, onboard a Missouri River steamship, Carson had an encounter that changed the course of his life. He met John C. Frémont, who told Carson he was on his way to the Rockies.

Portrait of James Beckwourth, from a photograph taken about 1868 —Courtesy Colorado Historical Society

Carson offered himself as a guide. Frémont and Carson's expeditions eventually made them both famous, and the two remained friends for life.

Jim Beckwourth, another rendezvous regular, knew the West from Missouri to California. His mountaineering life was full of adventures. The son of a white plantation manager and a black slave, he grew up with no schooling. For a time he lived with the Crow Indians and was honored as a chief. He and Baptiste got to know each other well and were friends for many years.

At the early rendezvous, only trappers, Indians, and traders came. Then outside merchants and travelers began to show up. Eventually the merely curious attended the meetings, along with emigrants passing through on their way to the Pacific coast—emigrants sometimes traveled with the trapping brigades for protection and guidance.

Among the early participants not involved in the fur trade was Sir William Drummond Stewart, who was at the 1834 meeting. Stewart, a Scot, made a number of visits to the West from 1833 on and attended the rendezvous simply because he enjoyed them. Jovial and generous, he was popular with the mountain men, who knew him as Captain Stewart. According to Kit Carson, he would be "forever remembered for his liberality and his many good qualities by the mountaineers who had the honor of his acquaintance." At the 1837 meeting Stewart was accompanied by an artist, Alfred Jacob Miller, who left excellent paintings and descriptions of the occasion.

Another onlooker at the 1834 rendezvous was Jason Lee, a Protestant missionary bound for the Oregon country. American missionaries began heading west in the 1830s hoping to convert the Indians to Christianity. Two such missionaries were present at the 1835 gathering, Samuel Parker and Dr. Marcus Whitman. A crowd watched as Dr. Whitman removed from Jim Bridger's back a Blackfoot arrowhead that had been lodged there for four years. When Whitman marveled that Bridger had had it in him for so long, Bridger is said to have told him, "Meat don't spoil in the mountains."

Whitman was at the rendezvous again a year later, this time with his new bride, Narcissa, and others. Narcissa Whitman and Eliza Spalding, another missionary wife, were the first white women to cross the Rocky Mountains. News that the women were coming to the rendezvous spread quickly, and their presence caused great excitement. The Indians had never seen white women. According to Dr. Whitman, they "were greatly interested with our females, cattle, and wagon." The Indian women were particularly fascinated with the clothes Mrs. Whitman and Mrs. Spalding wore.

The trappers were as much interested in the white women as were the Indians. Many of them had been away from society for years and had nearly forgotten how to act around ladies. The women were shocked at the trappers' noisemaking, all-night carousing, and gunplay, but the men showed them much respect and chivalrous attention. The religious services the missionaries held attracted quite a crowd. Other missionary families attended later rendezvous.

Captain Stewart's final rendezvous was in 1838. He and Baptiste would meet again in a few years. While there is no record of Baptiste's participation in the rendezvous after his first one, if he was at the 1838 meeting he might have encountered two of William Clark's sons, who, according to several accounts, were there.

The 1839 rendezvous was the last. By then, not only were the beaver nearly annihilated, but also demand for the fur dropped as fashions in men's hats changed from felt to silk. When they could no longer make a living as trappers, some of the mountain men became guides for visitors. Some settled down on farms. Others, Baptiste among them, found work as hunters supplying meat for trading posts.

The fur industry had depended on the mountain men. They explored the western territory and blazed its trails, ultimately opening the West to travelers and settlers. But Baptiste and the others did not see themselves as makers of history. They were simply fur men trying to make a living. In the process they had created a way of life like no other.

SEVEN

CHANGING TIMES AND NEW ADVENTURES

1839 TO 1843

Baptiste's next job was working as a hunter for Andrew Sublette, one of several brothers who had made names for themselves in the fur trade, and Louis Vasquez, an experienced and well-liked mountain man. In 1835 Sublette and Vasquez had built Fort Vasquez, a trading post on the South Platte River, near what is today Platteville, Colorado. Baptiste joined their thirty-two-man company when they left Independence, Missouri, in August 1839. He was one of two half-Indian men hired as hunters to supply meat for the men working at Fort Vasquez.

After the demise of the rendezvous, trading posts took over the role of meeting place and goods supplier for the trappers and Indians. As time went on, the posts, which were built throughout the West, also served missionaries, travelers, and emigrants. Although the posts were called forts, most of them were not military forts but fortified traders' camps. Some were permanent; others lasted only for a year or so. The buildings were made of logs or, where wood was scarce, of adobe, with fences eight to twelve feet high and thick walls to protect the men, livestock, and goods from Indian attacks.

Groomed buffalo hides, or robes, were replacing beaver skins as the preferred commodity in the fur trade. Indian women carefully cleaned and softened the hides to prepare them for sale. In return for the buffalo robes, as well as buffalo meat, the Indians received credit with which to buy paint, whiskey, knives, coffee, sugar, and other merchandise at the posts.

The food supplied to Baptiste's company on its way to Fort Vasquez, according to one of the men, E. Willard Smith, "consisted of bacon, and bread, made of flour and water formed into a paste and baked in a frying pan." The meat the hunters brought in was a welcome change from fried flour paste. "The hunter, Mr. Shabenare [Charbonneau], went out a short distance from the river to shoot a buffalo for his meat," wrote Smith.

The men reached Fort Vasquez in September. Baptiste's old friend Jim Beckwourth, who had worked for some years for Vasquez, had helped build the adobe fort. Vasquez, known as "old Vaskiss" (although he was not old), was a genial and popular host to his customers. He personally greeted old friends and new, and even brought in musicians and jugglers to entertain them.

Due to too much competition (and "too much frivolity," as one man said), Sublette and Vasquez did not prosper, and within a year of Baptiste's arrival they had decided to sell the post. Baptiste went to work for Charles Bent and Ceran St.

Vrain, proprietors of nearby Fort St. Vrain (as well as of the older Bent's Fort, farther south). In the spring of 1842 Baptiste was put in charge of a fleet of shallow-draft boats laden with robes for St. Louis. His crew included Jim Beckwourth, who brought along his new bride, Luisa Sandoval, a young woman from Santa Fe, then in Mexican territory.

When Baptiste and his crew set out, the South Platte River was so low that the boats got stuck on sandbars almost hourly. The boatmen struggled through the mud to push the crafts ahead. When this failed, they unloaded the cargo and lugged it and the empty boats along the shore to the next navigable water. After traveling thus for forty-five miles, they could no longer move forward. They were stranded.

Baptiste ordered his crew to set up camp on a small strip of land in the middle of the river. He called the island St. Helena, for the island where Napoleon was exiled from 1815 to 1821. Perhaps he thought it appropriate to name his tiny refuge for a place associated with the man responsible for the Louisiana Purchase, which had given further incentive to the Corps of Discovery's voyage.

Baptiste was far from lonely on the island. Beckwourth entertained the stranded boatmen with his stories of hairbreadth escapes from danger, stories in which he was always the hero. For his tall tales, Beckwourth had earned a reputation as a "gaudy liar." Passing travelers visited the camp as well. One was John C. Frémont, a lieutenant in the U.S. Corps of Topographical Engineers, who came by in July. His guide, Baptiste's

John C. Frémont
—Courtesy Henry E.
Huntington Library
and Art Gallery

friend Kit Carson, had gone ahead, but Frémont stayed a while to enjoy Baptiste's hospitality.

Frémont was part of another change in the West, the rise of government-sponsored scientific and mapmaking expeditions. Although the mountain men had blazed trails and named rivers, mountains, and landmarks, no reliable maps had yet been made. Frémont had been sent west to make some. Many Americans firmly believed that the United States had a natural right to claim all the land to the Pacific coast, and to help accomplish this, it was necessary to mark the best routes for settlers.

Frémont's journal describes his visit to Baptiste's island camp. The tents were pitched in a grove of very large cottonwoods. "Smoke was arising from the scattered fires, and the encampment had quite a patriarchal air. Mr. Chabonard received us hospitably. One of the people was sent to gather mint, with the aid of which he concocted very good julep; and some boiled buffalo tongue, and coffee with the luxury of sugar, were soon set before us."

A month after Frémont's visit to St. Helena, another traveler, Rufus B. Sage, arrived. Sage was as surprised and impressed as Frémont had been to find Baptiste "a gentleman of superior information." Sage's comments offer further documentation of Baptiste's charm and intelligence:

> [Charbonneau] had acquired a classic education and could converse quite fluently in German, Spanish, French, and English, as well as several Indian languages. His mind, also, was well stored with choice reading, and enriched by extensive travel and observation. Having visited most of the important places . . . in England, France, and Germany, he knew how to turn his experience to good advantage.
>
> There was a quaint humor and shrewdness in his conversation, so garbed with intelligence and perspicuity, that he at once insinuated himself into the good graces of listeners, and commanded their admiration and respect.

It is not known exactly how or when Baptiste and his crew got off the island, but by the spring of 1843, Baptiste was back in St. Louis. The city was quite changed from the place Baptiste remembered from his school days. The fur trade had given rise to a prosperous economy, and the population had multiplied. Successful merchants lived in beautiful large homes, and the city's wealthy families entertained at teas, balls, and parties. Theater and the arts flourished. Part of the Louisiana Territory had been named the Missouri Territory, and in 1821 it had become the State of Missouri.

Baptiste probably went unrecognized while in town. He could not pay a visit to his famous mentor, William Clark, who had died in 1838. Baptiste may have hoped to find his father, however, or at least get word of him, but it is unknown whether he was successful. Their last documented meeting had been twenty years earlier, at the Curtis and Woods trading post.

After Toussaint left St. Louis with Sacagawea for Fort Manuel in 1811, his whereabouts for some time were unknown. On April 19 of that year he was sent deep into the Northwest wilderness to find a certain trapping expedition and was not heard from for several years. Some believed he was captured by the British during the War of 1812 and held prisoner. Another theory speculates that in his travels he strayed into Mexican territory and was imprisoned there.

In 1816 Toussaint was back in St. Louis, where he took a position with the Indian Department as a guide and interpreter. Very likely he received the appointment thanks to General Clark's influence. In addition to his assignment with Duke Paul, Toussaint served the famous Maximilian, Prince of Wied-Neuwied; prominent military leaders General Henry Atkinson and Colonel Henry Leavenworth; and renowned artists Karl Bodmer and George Catlin. Of Toussaint, "Old Charbonneau," Maximilian wrote, "He had five names among [the Hidatsa], the chief of the little village; the man who possesses many gourds; the great horse from abroad; the forest bear; and the fifth, which . . . is not very refined."

Toussaint was in St. Louis again in 1839 to collect his final wages from the Indian Department. Records describe him on that occasion as "tottering under the infirmities of eighty winters, without a dollar to support him." He had escaped the dreadful smallpox epidemic that had spread through Indian country in 1837–38 and destroyed almost every soul in the Mandan and Hidatsa villages. It must have been painful for Baptiste to hear of that tragedy befalling his childhood home. By the time Baptiste reached St. Louis in 1843, his father had again dropped out of sight.

The town at this time was bustling with activity. Almost a thousand emigrants bound for Oregon were forming wagon parties and purchasing goods for their journey. A famous naturalist and artist, John James Audubon, was preparing for his own trip west. And John C. Frémont was gathering an outfit for his second mapping expedition, again to be guided by Kit Carson.

Sir William Drummond Stewart, nineteenth Lord of Grandtully and seventh Baronet of Murthly, Scotland, was also organizing an expedition into the Rockies. He was the man whom Baptiste and the other mountain men knew from the rendezvous as Captain Stewart. At that time he had been living on a retired British army officer's pay. But in 1838 he succeeded his brother to a noble title and large estates, and he could now return to the Rockies in grand style. This trip was not to be a serious expedition but a great pleasure trip. Sir William hired Baptiste to drive one of the wagons.

Once assembled, Sir William's group consisted of some sixty men—drivers, hunters, trappers, and guides, along with the gentlemen adventurers the nobleman had invited. Several were friends from eastern cities, others from New Orleans and even Havana, Cuba. He also invited some of the prominent young men of St. Louis, among them relatives of General Clark—his youngest son, Jefferson Clark; his stepson John Radford; and a nephew, William Clark Kennerly. The famous Father Pierre Jean De Smet and two other Jesuit priests, as well as a journalist and several scientists, also joined Sir William's company for part of the trip.

Each guest provided his own horse and a manservant. The men dressed in flannel shirts, corduroy trousers, and heavy boots with spurs, and they each carried a rifle, a pistol, and a hunting knife. For every six men there was a two-wheeled cart, or *charette*, loaded with gear and hitched to two mules. It was one of these *charettes* that Baptiste was to drive.

William Sublette, brother of Baptiste's former boss Andrew Sublette, was the chief guide for Sir William's expedition. He wrote that the men of the company were "doctors, lawyers, botanists, bug catchers, hunters and men of nearly all professions." When Sir William learned that John James Audubon was in St. Louis, he eagerly invited him to join the expedition. Audubon declined, disclosing privately that he thought the party had "too many people of too many sorts. [Sir William] takes sixteen days provisions only, and then depends on dried buffalo meat for the rest of the journey." Audubon said he found Sir William "a very curious character."

*Portrait of Sir
William
Drummond
Stewart by
Alfred J. Miller*
—Courtesy Gilcrease
Museum

The company left St. Louis on May 2, 1843, and headed up the Platte River valley. Sublette was too experienced a mountaineer to treat the trip as a carefree frolic. He knew that there were plenty of dangers to watch out for, especially when so many of the group were greenhorns. He organized the party in semimilitary order. At night they drew their wagons into a circle and most of the men slept under the vehicles, with their saddles as pillows. Sir William had the men pitch his elegant tent nightly, but the others used tents only when it rained. Guards kept watch at night.

On the first night, rain fell in torrents, and it continued to rain day after day. The rivers were overflowing, and the company was often drenched. They could not keep fires going and had to eat cold rations, standing ankle-deep in water. Some of the men decided they had had enough of the adventure and went back to St. Louis.

After the rains stopped, spirits rose. The men amused themselves with footsraces, horse races, and other tests of skill. They shot buffalo, more for sport than for meat, taking only the best parts, the hump and the tongue, and leaving the carcasses to rot on the plains. They visited Indian camps, where Jefferson Clark's red hair often made him welcome, for some of the Indians remembered his father, William Clark, whom they had called the Red-headed Chief.

William Clark Kennerly's memoirs noted that the Stewart party traveled over some of the same country the Corps of Discovery had visited, and that Baptiste was "by a singular coincidence, again to make the journey and guide the son of William Clark through the same region." Asked whether Baptiste spoke of his mother and "if he seemed to appreciate her fortitude and courage in making possible the discovery of an inland route to the great Pacific," Kennerly replied that Baptiste "spoke more often of the mules he was driving and might have been heard early and late expatiating in not too complimentary a manner on their stubbornness."

There was plenty of liquor on the trip, and sometimes the merrymaking turned to brawling. One day a fight broke out between two of the men. Apparently Baptiste enjoyed a good scuffle. According to Kennerly, "Charboneau ran excitedly about, keeping a ring around the fighters with his heavy whip and shouting for no one to interfere. It was not a very even fight; Smith was much the larger man, but, after a few rounds when he jumped on Walker's back in an effort to bear him to the ground, Walker drew his pistol and, firing over his shoulder, wounded Smith in the thigh, the wonder being that he did not kill him."

The party had other troubles as well. Indians stole some of the horses. One man was lost for several days and almost starved while wandering the plains. Another man accidently shot and killed himself. The men were nearly trampled by a tremendous herd of buffalo. Later they ran short of provisions, and many members turned back. The trip was a disappointment to Stewart, who was saddened by the changes he saw on what was once wild frontier.

Baptiste left before the expedition ended. By August 14, 1843, he was back in St. Louis, perhaps having received the news of his father's death. A promissory note of that date reads:

> *I promise to pay to J. B. Chabonno the sum of three hundred and twenty dollars, as soon as I dispose of land claimed by him said Charbonno from the estate of his deceased father.*

> *St. Louis August 14, 1843*
> *Francis Pinsoneau*

The exact time and place of Toussaint's death is not recorded. Three days later Baptiste endorsed the note over to William Sublette, perhaps to cash it. The land had been Toussaint's reward for service during the Lewis and Clark expedition thirty-seven years earlier.

Not only had Baptiste no family left, it must have been clear to him that an era had ended. The trails once known only to Indians and trappers were becoming mapped roads with well-stocked forts and trading posts to serve travelers. The great western migration had begun, with thousands of men, women, and children heading west to start farms and settlements in Oregon and California. (The former was jointly owned by the United States and Britain at the time; the latter was claimed by Mexico.)

Baptiste soon joined a caravan headed back to the mountains. The following winter Baptiste signed on again to work as a hunter for his former employers Ceran St. Vrain and Charles Bent, this time at Bent's Fort, on the Arkansas River.

EIGHT

BENT'S FORT HUNTER

1843 TO 1846

 Bent and St. Vrain established Bent's Fort about 1843. The fort was on the Santa Fe Trail, close to what was then the Mexican border, in present La Junta, Colorado. The post employed some one 150 men, many as hunters to supply meat not only for the workers but also for traders, trappers, and visitors who came there.

Upon his arrival in the winter of late 1843, Baptiste found that the fort was not a dull and isolated outpost but a very busy trade center on the Santa Fe Trail. Though the trade in beaver pelts was drying up, in its place came buffalo robes from the north and merchandise from Mexico. Almost daily, great wagons filled with gold, silver, and furs rolled in from Chihuahua and Santa Fe; from the East came cutlery, hats, cloth, and hardware for exchange. In addition, emigrants headed to Oregon and California stopped at the fort to replenish their supplies, and there was brisk trade with nearby Indians and trappers as well.

Bent's Fort was "civilized." The American flag flew above its walls. The Sabbath was observed. The men ate their meals at a

Drawing of Bent's Fort by Charles M. Russell, showing the Indians requesting permission to enter —Courtesy Amon Carter Museum

table, with knives and forks. It was an easy life for Baptiste, who at thirty-nine was no longer an energetic youth. After his day's hunt he was assured of a bed, good meals, and pay of a dollar a day. For the first time in many years he had leisure to rest, read, and enjoy the diverse company of those who lived in the fort and an ever-changing flow of visitors.

Friendly tribes, especially the Arapaho and the Cheyenne, often camped near the fort. Bent and St. Vrain avoided trouble by treating the Indians fairly and refusing to sell them whiskey. Kit Carson had worked at the fort from 1840 to 1842 and spoke of the kindness of Bent and St. Vrain: "I can only say that their equals were never before seen in the mountains." Of St. Vrain, he said, "All the mountaineers considered him their best friend and treated him with the greatest respect."

Many mountain men came through Bent's Fort at one time or another. In the evenings they swapped tales of their adventures such as enduring Indian attacks, encountering grizzlies, and getting lost in the wilderness. Baptiste whiled away many hours playing cards with Bill Guerrier, an interpreter for the Cheyenne. Guerrier had learned to communicate with the tribe by copying their expressive gestures, and he taught Baptiste their sign language.

William Boggs, son of the governor of Missouri, visited the fort in 1844. His notes mentioned Baptiste. He said he had learned much from the hunters, particularly Baptiste. "This Baptiste Charbenau," he wrote, "was the small papoose, or half-breed of the elder Charbenau that was employed by the Lewis and Clark expedition. He had been educated to some extent; he wore his hair long—that hung down to his shoulders. It was said that Charbenau was the best man on foot on the plains or in the Rocky Mountains."

Boggs's journal also refers to a young half-French, half-Indian man called "Tessou," who "was in some way related to Charbenou." Tessou (Toussaint, Jr.?) may have been Baptiste's half-brother—Toussaint Charbonneau had had many wives. St. Vrain made Tessou leave Bent's Fort after he shot at one of the fort's blacksmiths.

John C. Frémont came through the fort in 1844, returning from his second mapping expedition. This time he had gone as far as California with Kit Carson. Frémont's 1845 report contained enthusiastic descriptions of the rich land of California. The published report became a best-seller, and emigrants used it as a travel guide to the West. Frémont stopped at Bent's Fort again on his third expedition, which Carson again guided. This time Frémont had with him sixty armed men and a cannon. Trouble was brewing.

One of the men with Frémont, Lieutenant J. W. Abert, another Topographical Corps engineer, remained at the fort for some days. Baptiste invited him to visit the Cheyenne, and they watched the women perform a dance, which Abert sketched. The engineer also made drawings of Bent's Fort. The fort was made of sun-dried adobe bricks, built strongly for protection against invaders. The walls were three to four feet thick and fourteen feet high, flanked by two eighteen-foot-high towers. At the center was a large courtyard, and around the perimeter were rooms for storage and housing. There was a well to provide clean water and an icehouse for keeping fresh food.

In 1846 the shadow of war descended upon this busy and peaceful community. The governor of New Mexico (then part of Mexico), Manuel Armijo, was not friendly toward Americans. He taxed everyone crossing into Mexico and charged high duties on goods brought into the country. The Mexican government imposed limits on international trade, prohibiting the importation of some goods as well as the exportation of gold and silver. These regulations cost both American and Mexican traders a great deal of money, and many protested.

Another underlying cause of the United States' dispute with Mexico was the American desire for more land, including California, New Mexico (which then included what is now Arizona), and Texas. This area had changed hands several times. Until 1821 it was a Spanish possession, along with the rest of Mexico. Then Mexico declared independence from Spain and took over the government. The United States wanted to buy the land, but Mexico was not willing to sell it. A number of Americans had already settled in California. Some of them had taken Mexican citizenship to obtain land grants; a few had married the daughters of wealthy Mexican ranchers.

Texans also had a quarrel with Mexico. In 1836, Texas had declared itself a free republic, but Mexico never recognized its independence. During the struggles of that year, Mexico's bloody siege of the Alamo left Texans particularly embittered. Texas became a state in 1845, but Mexico disputed America's claim to the region. Finally, in the spring of 1846, the border conflicts combined with the complaints of the traders led to an official grievance from the United States, which in turn sparked a war with Mexico.

In June 1846, early in the war, Colonel Stephen Watts Kearny marched through Bent's Fort with five companies of the First Dragoons. The dragoons were mounted soldiers, specially trained and heavily armed. Kearny had orders to lead the Army of the West to Santa Fe and then to California. He was a strong commander, accustomed to frontier service. The previous year he had traveled the Oregon Trail to South Pass and the Santa Fe Trail from Bent's Fort to the settlements on the Missouri.

(Kearny was also related to William Clark, having married Mary Radford, daughter of Clark's second wife.)

Following Kearny's arrival, the First Missouri Volunteers rode into the fort. They were to serve in Mexico under Colonel Doniphan. Major Meriwether Lewis Clark (eldest son of William Clark) and his cousin, Sergeant William Clark Kennerly (who had been on Sir William's expedition with Baptiste), were with the artillery corps.

Kennerly's memoirs record how bravely the volunteer corps had marched out of Fort Leavenworth in Missouri, dressed in uniforms of blue with red standing collars and wearing gold-braided caps. They carried large knives in their belts, and some had revolvers. By the time they reached Bent's Fort, those dashing uniforms were in tatters and they had lost half their horses. Kennerly did not mention Baptiste's presence at the fort, and possibly Baptiste did not recognize the two ragged and weary soldiers as old acquaintances.

Along with all the soldiers, a large number of Santa Fe traders and freight wagons were halted near the fort, ordered not to cross the Arkansas River ahead of the army. The fort was crowded beyond its capacity with people and animals, filled with noise and commotion. One observer found the post "excessively crowded. . . . Here were many races and colors—a confusion of tongues, of rank and condition, and of cross purposes. Meanwhile the long column of horses continually passed, fording the river; but officers were collecting stragglers, and straggling themselves."

In August Colonel Kearny and his troops left Bent's Fort for Santa Fe. It is not clear whether Baptiste left the fort with the dragoons or Kearny sent for him later, but he would soon be put to work for the United States Army.

The soldiers' presence had disrupted trade at Bent's Fort, and the supplies they took were never even paid for. One of the last visitors to Bent's Fort in this momentous year was Francis Parkman, an easterner traveling, he said, "on a tour of curiosity and amusement." He arrived soon after the army had left and described the atmosphere:

> It seemed as if a swarm of locusts had invaded the country. The grass for miles around was cropped close by General Kearney's soldiery. When we came to the fort, we found that not only had the horses eaten up the grass, but their owners had made way with the stores of the little trading post; so that we had great difficulty in procuring the few articles which we required for our homeward journey. The army was gone, the life and bustle passed away, and the fort was a scene of dull and lazy tranquility.

NINE

THE LONG MARCH

1846 to 1847

 On August 15, 1846, Colonel Kearny issued a proclamation claiming for the United States most of the province of New Mexico. On August 19 Kearny's army took over Santa Fe. The Mexican inhabitants offered no resistance; they had long been friendly neighbors, with no desire to fight. Kearny established a civil government there, appointing Charles Bent, Baptiste's boss at Bent's fort, governor. (Bent was murdered by Indians the following January.) Meanwhile, the Missouri Volunteers marched to Chihuahua, where they fought bravely until the war in northern Mexico ended in 1847.

After his bloodless conquest of New Mexico, Kearny was promoted to brigadier general. He now had orders to go on to California and claim all the land as far as the Pacific Ocean for the United States. His three hundred dragoons, with two mobile cannons and many supply wagons, would begin their march in September. General Kearny arranged to bring cattle for meat on the long journey and hired hunters to supplement the beef with game. The general also hired guides, or scouts, to lead the way.

Due to his skills as a frontiersman, as well as his knowledge of languages, Baptiste was chosen to be one of Kearny's guides and hunters for the march. Baptiste's fellow mountain man Thomas Fitzpatrick was General Kearny's chief guide. Two other mountaineer friends, Antoine Leroux and Antoine Robidoux, also served as scouts and hunters. Leroux, after a long career as a trapper, had established a trading business in Santa Fe. Robidoux had recently abandoned trapping because of the increase in Indian hostilities.

Baptiste had heard something about California from the few trappers who had ventured that far. Jedediah Smith was the first white American to reach the coast from the east. He led a group of seventeen trappers into the territory in 1826. His party was graciously received by Franciscan fathers at the San Gabriel Mission, in present Claremont, near Los Angeles. The Mexican governor was less hospitable; he ordered Smith's men out of the country. Smith returned to tell about California's lofty mountains, green valleys, streams and rivers teeming with fish and beaver, and woods full of deer, elk, and bear.

Kit Carson had been in California many times, and he also spoke of its beauty. Joseph Reddeford Walker, with a group of seventeen men, blazed a trail in 1833 across the Great Basin and through the Sierra Nevada. With him was Zenas Leonard, whose journal recounts a visit to an enchanted valley enclosed by steep cliffs with great waterfalls—they had discovered the Yosemite Valley. Leonard also wrote of giant trees, some as high as 350 feet with a spread of over 100 feet. Modern visitors can see trees like these at Sequoia National Park.

Baptiste was eager to visit this wonderful place. Making the journey across the Southwest with Kearny's forces would be a good deal safer than going with a small party. But it would not be free of danger. The Mexican authorities did not welcome outsiders, and Indians sometimes attacked travelers as well. The deserts were difficult to cross; both water and game were scarce there.

All the guides had some experience with desert travel, but none, except possibly Robidoux, had crossed the entire route to California. Their task was to choose a path where wagons could pass and where there was enough water and grass for the horses and mules. In addition to the harsh desert, the mountainous areas were difficult if not impossible to pass with heavily loaded wagons. Much depended on the skills of Baptiste and the other guides.

Lieutenant W. H. Emory, an engineer with Kearny's command and the mapmaker for the journey, recognized Baptiste's abilities. "I saw some objects," he wrote, "perched on the hills to the west, which were at first mistaken for large cedars, but dwindled by distance to a shrub. Chaboneau (one of our guides) exclaimed 'Indians! There are the Apaches.' His more practiced eye detected human figures in my shrubbery."

Not long after the troops left Santa Fe, traveling south along the Rio Grande, there was a change in plan. General Kearny received word that a battalion of Mormon volunteers had been ordered to meet in Santa Fe and follow Kearny to California. The general assigned Lieutenant Colonel Philip St. George

Cooke to lead the Mormon Battalion and bring them to join his dragoons as soon as possible.

The Mormons who made up the battalion had joined the army to get to California and help build a community there. The Mormons, hated and feared by many because their religion was different, had been driven from their homes in Illinois and elsewhere. They sought a new home in the West where they could live in peace and have their own government.

The Mormons who gathered in Santa Fe in October 1846 were not experienced soldiers or hardened frontiersmen, but rather entire families, including women and children, hoping to start settlements in California. The "army" consisted of 536 men and 36 women. Some were men too old and feeble to march, let alone fight; others were mere boys. The men who were fit for service were untrained and not used to army discipline. To make matters worse, Colonel Cooke had no supplies to issue and few mules. Kearny's Army of the West had cleaned everything out.

Cooke was an experienced commander, a graduate of West Point with a long career of service in the West. But he had never before faced a challenge as tough as this. Everything seemed against his chances of success. He had been advised to take rations for one hundred days, but he was unable to find enough teams to haul more than sixty days' supply. He took all the flour, sugar, coffee, salt, salt pork, and soap he could get in Santa Fe, but it was not enough for the journey.

Cooke trimmed the troops down to 387 of the most able men. He reluctantly allowed five women, wives of officers, to remain with the battalion, but they had to furnish their own transportation and necessities. He led his poorly supplied and undisciplined battalion out of Santa Fe on October 19. Only the officers and guides had horses or mules; the others would make the journey on foot. They could not foresee that before they reached California, things would become much worse. And Baptiste would be with them.

Colonel Philip St. George Cooke, leader of the Mormon Battalion
—Courtesy Latter-day Saints Church Archives

Some days after General Kearny learned of the Mormon Battalion's intention to join him, a party of fifteen horsemen approached the general from the west, led by Kit Carson. Carson was carrying dispatches to Washington, D.C., with astonishing news. American settlers in California had revolted against Mexican authority. Led by Baptiste's old acquaintance John C. Frémont and others, the settlers, the message said, had already claimed California for the United States.

Kearny was eager to get to the scene of the action without delay, to lend support and oversee the newly conquered territory. Since Carson knew the way, the general ordered him to turn around and guide the army to Los Angeles. Carson agreed reluctantly, as he had hoped to visit his family on the way to Washington. Kearny ordered his guide Thomas Fitzpatrick to deliver the dispatches in Carson's place.

Carson warned Kearny that at his present rate of travel it would take his army four months to reach its destination. Kearny decided to reduce his company to one hundred men and march them through quickly. He gave up the wagons and sent for packsaddles to carry supplies on the mules and horses. He ordered Baptiste and some of the other guides to go farther south and explore a route suitable for Colonel Cooke's wagons. They were then to guide the Mormon Battalion to California.

Baptiste scouted a path before meeting the battalion in Albuquerque on October 24. Colonel Cooke wrote that he recommended "a route different in part and farther than that taken by the general." The other guides also advised a detour.

To allow access for the wagons and teams, the route would take Cooke and his party three hundred miles south.

It was the beginning of an epic journey, a march of 104 days across deserts prickly with cactus, over boulder-strewn hills, through narrow canyons, and up steep mountains. The flinty ground soon wore out the heaviest boots. The only available substitutes were moccasins, and cactus spines cut right through them.

Cooke had let his men know from the start that they were soldiers, subject to military discipline. There was to be no sleeping on guard, no stealing from the food wagons, no disobeying orders. The men thought him very strict, but they did their work, marching with heavy packs on their backs over the rough ground. Sometimes they had to help the mules get the wagons through heavy sand by pulling on long ropes, twenty men to a wagon.

The soldiers suffered from the burning sun and the meager rations. Although army discipline was new to them, they were bound to one another by ties of religion and friendship, and they were obedient to their own leaders. They worked willingly and hard, and they drank no alcohol. Soon they became used to the routine and gained respect for Cooke.

Baptiste ranged ahead, scouting for the best path, seeking water, and hunting for deer and bear. He traveled many more miles than did the troops, riding a mule—not his favorite mount. One day after a hard ride, Baptiste's mule seemed worn out. He stopped to give it a rest, and when he attempted to mount it again it kicked at him and ran off. He followed it for a couple of miles and then shot it, partly from anger and partly to retrieve his saddle and pistols. The camp was amused when he walked in carrying his saddle.

The battalion followed the Rio Grande south and crossed mountains to the west, just missing Guadalupe Pass. They crossed the mountains over a thousand-foot-high rim. The trail was so narrow they used shovels and picks to widen it, then worked the wagons down the face of the rim by means of ropes and manpower. According to one of the men, "I think no other man but Cook would even [have] attempted to cross such a place but he seemed to have the spirit and energy of a [Napoleon Bonaparte]."

Baptiste and the other scouts spent much of their time looking for water in the desert. Sometimes Baptiste left messages attached to sticks for the battalion: "No water. Charbonneau." Cooke wrote of one unhappy occasion: "Water was found, but it was not enough for the men to drink; it was soon gone, and the poor fellows were waiting for it to leak from the rocks, and dipping it with spoons!" Once they went three days without water.

Near the Gila River the battalion found mules and supplies that General Kearny had left behind for them. The general had also sent them a message from Warner's Ranch in California, with a Mexican guide to show them good places to camp and to find grass and water. At last the weary men crossed the Colorado River into California, on January 9, 1847. This knowledge lifted their spirits. Cooke allowed them to rest, then had them clean up their weapons and stand inspection.

Though they looked like ragtag vagabonds, their bearing was that of proud soldiers.

In the meantime, Baptiste and four others had been sent ahead to find General Kearny. They were to tell him of the battalion's approach and ask for more mules. Baptiste returned with news that two of the scouts stayed behind "lest they might fall into the hands of the hostile Californians [Mexicans], who, it seemed, held a grudge against them."

Sketch of the junction of the Gila and Colorado Rivers by John R. Bartlett. Across the river lay California, the destination of the Mormon Battalion and their guides. —Courtesy California State Library

JUNCTION OF THE GILA AND COLORADO RIVERS, LOOKING UP THE GILA.

On January 21 the battalion reached Warner's Ranch. It was the first settlement they had seen in California. "Here we had the first full meal," wrote one of the volunteers. They learned that Kearny's force had rested here for a few days, then gone on, only to be ambushed by Mexicans at the Indian town of San Pasqual. A disastrous battle had followed. Eighteen of Kearny's men were killed and many wounded, including Kearny himself.

Major Emory described the morning after the battle: "Day dawned on the most tattered and ill-fed detachment of men that ever the United States mustered under her colors. . . . Our provisions were exhausted, our horses dead, our mules on their last legs, and our men, now reduced to one-third of their number, were ragged, worn-down by fatigue, and emaciated." Eventually Kearny's men were rescued and the tide of the war turned.

At Warner's Ranch, Cooke's men were ordered to go to San Diego instead of Los Angeles. This meant crossing the Chocolate Mountains and the Imperial Valley toward the coast, a hard march. On January 27 they reached the mission of San Luis Rey. Corporal Tyler described the soldiers' feelings:

> *One mile below the mission, we ascended a bluff, when the long-looked for great Pacific Ocean appeared plain to our view, only about three miles distant. The joy, the cheer that filled our souls, none but worn-out pilgrims nearing a haven of rest can imagine. We had talked about and sung of the "the great Pacific sea," and we were now upon its very borders, and its beauty far exceeded our most sanguine expectations.*

Baptiste no doubt shared the soldiers' joy and awe. Cooke thanked Baptiste and the other guides for their work and dismissed them from service. The battalion marched on to San Diego, where they arrived sunburned, hungry, ragged, and barefoot—but, according to Tyler, cheerful: "The crowning satisfaction of all to us was that we had succeeded in making the great national highway across the American desert."

The two-thousand-mile journey was the longest infantry march in United States history. Two railroad lines and a much-used highway were later built on the trail it had made. The Mormon Battalion, however, never fired a shot in the war.

On February 2, 1848, Mexico ceded to the United States what are now the states of California, Texas, New Mexico, and Arizona. It was the beginning of a new era for America, and of a new life for Baptiste. From now on, California would be his home.

TEN

CALIFORNIA YEARS AND THE END OF THE TRAIL

1847 TO 1866

On November 24, 1847, Baptiste took office as an alcalde (a public administrator and judge) at the San Luis Rey Mission. The California governor had recommended him for the post because he had a reputation for trustworthiness and because he spoke Spanish, a language that the Indians at the mission understood.

San Luis Rey was one of many California missions built along the Pacific coast by Franciscan priests hoping to convert the local natives to Christianity. The San Luis Rey Mission, about five miles from the ocean, was the most beautiful and extensive of them all. Its great cathedral, which could hold a thousand worshippers, had vaulted ceilings and elaborate carvings and was surrounded by gracefully arched walkways. Baptiste had not seen such a beautiful building since his days in Europe.

Under the Franciscans, the mission had thrived. Its fields were fertile and well watered, and its orchards spread over acres. The church owned thousands of cattle, sheep, goats,

Watercolor of the San Luis Rey Mission, 1848, by William R. Hutton
—Courtesy Henry E. Huntington Library and Art Gallery

pigs, horses, and mules. In 1836 almost three thousand Native Americans had lived there, working the fields and orchards and studying with the priests.

By the time Baptiste arrived in 1847, however, the mission was almost deserted and its buildings were falling into disrepair. The Mexican government had taken title to the property in 1836. Mexican ranchers had taken over the land, as well as the cattle and sheep. The priests were forced to leave, and the Indians moved into the foothills nearby. Many of them survived by working for the ranchers.

John Bidwell, an early American settler in California, was known for treating the Indians fairly and won many of them over to the American cause during the war. When California became American territory, Bidwell was appointed to protect the San Luis Rey Mission property and look after the rights of the Indians there. But because of the hostility of the ranchers, he soon left.

Baptiste's duties were similar to Bidwell's. As soon as he took office he found the situation of the Indian laborers at the mission deplorable. They were much like slaves of the ranchers, with no property of their own. They were dependent on their employers for food, shelter, and schooling. The wealthy landowners controlled both their wages and the prices they paid for food and supplies. Most of the Indians had lived at the mission since infancy, and they did not have the skills to live off the land like other Native Americans.

One landowner, Jose Pico, who ran a store at the mission, came to Baptiste with a bill for $51.37 for whiskey and other goods he had sold to an Indian laborer, demanding that Baptiste force the man to pay. According to the law, Baptiste was obliged to sentence the laborer, whose pay was twelve and a half cents a day, to work for Pico until the debt was paid. Because the man had little chance ever to pay off his debt, the sentence was equivalent to slavery.

Baptiste's entries in the mission account books and a letter, written in Spanish, are the only writings of his that have survived. The letter, dated May 9, 1848, requested Pico to send a

This is to certify that Ifigenia
after a fair settlement it appears a balance
Due Don Jose Ant. Pico of fifty one Dollars and thirty
seven and a half Cents. all Acct. settled before me
at this office at St Louis Rey April 24th 1848

J B Charbonneau
alc

P. J. B. Charbonneau do sentence Ifigenia to work
in the service of Don Jose Ant. Pico at the rate of
twelve and a half Cents per Day, untill he (Ifigenia)
has paid said Debt.

at this Magistrates office St Louis Rey
April 24th 1848

J B Charbonneau
alc

Señor Amigo Mio:
Don Jose Ant. Pico —

Los Indios de las Flores quieren que Vd.
le ace el favor de Despachar algunos Bagueros;
a huntar su Ganado por aca si acas que aber
algunos De ellas a las Pulgas.

San Luis Rey Mayo y 7 de 1848

J B Charbonneau
alc
3. P

few of his cowboys to help find some Indians' missing cattle. No reply is recorded.

Baptiste found it difficult to get along with the ranchers, who resented his sympathy for the Indians. In July 1848, less than a year after taking office, he decided that he could no longer enforce such unfair regulations. He resigned, giving as his reason: "a half-breed Indian of the U.S. is regarded by the people as favoring the Indians more than he should do, and hence there is much complaint against him."

A few months later, Baptiste rode north to Sacramento. A man named James Marshall had discovered gold near there on January 24, 1848. As soon as news of the discovery got out, men began to flock to California in search of the precious metal. Soldiers left their posts, sailors abandoned ships, and merchants closed up shops to join the gold rush.

Upon reaching the Sierra Nevada foothills, Baptiste settled in a spot called Murderer's Bar, on the Middle Fork of the American River. The place was named in memory of a brutal murder that had been committed among its earliest settlers. Baptiste set up camp on the bar, which was lined with willows and smooth-barked alders, and tried panning for gold in the river.

An English traveler, Frank Marryat, described Murderer's Bar in 1851, while Baptiste was living there:

Immediately beneath us the swift river glided tranquilly, though foaming still from the great battle which, a few yards higher up, it had fought with a mass of black obstructing rocks. On the banks was a village of canvas that the winter rains had bleached to perfection, and round it the miners were at work at every point. Many were waist-deep in the water, toiling in bands to construct a race and dam to turn the river's course; others were entrenched in holes, like grave-diggers, working down to the "bed rock." Some were on the brink of the stream washing out "prospects" from tin pans or wooden "batteas"; and others worked in company with the long-tom, by means of water-sluices artfully conveyed from the river. Many were coyote-ing in subterranean holes, from which from time to time their heads popped out, like those of squirrels, to take a look at the world, and a few with drills, dissatisfied with nature's work, were preparing to remove large rocks with gunpowder. All was life, merriment, vigor, and determination, as this part of the earth was being turned inside out to see what it was made of. . . .

One would ask how it is that Murderer's Bar, despite its name, is a peaceable village, where each man's wealth, in the shape of ten feet square of soil, is virtuously respected by his neighbor; it is not because there is enough for all, for every paying claim has long ago been appropriated, and the next comer must go further on. There is a justice of the peace (up to his arms in the river just at present), and there is a constable (who has been "prospecting" a bag of earth from the hill, and been rewarded with a gold flake of the value of three cents); these two, one would suppose, could scarcely control two or three hundred men, with rude passions and quick tempers, each of whom, as you observe, carries his revolver even while at work. But these armed, rough-looking fellows themselves elected their judge and constable, and stand, ever ready, as "specials," to support them.

Baptiste's old friend Jim Beckwourth met him at Murderer's Bar and stayed with him through the winter of 1849–50. Beckwourth had made three previous journeys to California, in 1835, 1839, and 1845. Later he discovered the pass over the Sierra now named for him.

Others known to Baptiste came to northern California during this period. In 1850 John Radford and William Clark Kennerly came with a group from St. Louis to try their luck at mining. Radford took part in a battle to oust some squatters who had camped on early California settler John Sutter's property in Sacramento. Radford was wounded by gunfire and cared for at Sutter's Fort.

Duke Paul was also in California in 1850, visiting Sutter at his ranch on the Feather River. As he watched some young Shoshoni men thresh wheat, he recalled his old friend Baptiste. He noted in his journal, "Among these [workers] was a handsome youth, quite intelligent, who reminded me strangely and with a certain sadness, on account of his startling likeness, of a lad from the same tribe whom I took to Europe with me from a fur-trading post at the mouth of the Kansas, in western Mississippi, in the fall of 1823, and who was my companion there on all my travels over Europe and northern Africa until 1829, when he returned with me to America." The prince obviously did not know that his friend was at that very moment living not far away.

Although he never struck it rich, Baptiste remained in the Sacramento Valley until he was in his late fifties. For a time he made his home in Secret Ravine, near Auburn, California. Secret Ravine was an old mining camp in a beautiful canyon. In 1861 Baptiste began working as a clerk at the Orleans Hotel in Auburn. After the hard labor of mining, it must have

Woodcut of the Orleans Hotel, Auburn, California, from Thompson & West's History of Placer County —Courtesy California State Library

been a relief to have a "desk job." He had many friends, who probably enjoyed listening to his tales of life as a mountain man. One of his friends described him as "of pleasant manners, intelligent, well read in the topics of the day, and was generally esteemed in the community."

During his years in northern California, Baptiste saw many changes in his growing community. California became a state in 1850. Houses, schools, and businesses were established, Wells Fargo coaches came through regularly, and immigrants from China took up residence. Even after gold fever cooled, the area's fertile land and pleasant climate continued to attract settlers.

In the spring of 1866 Baptiste felt the desire to move on, after he heard of newly discovered goldfields in the Montana Territory. Montana was Shoshoni country, his mother's homeland. At sixty-one, Baptiste was not as strong as he had been. Perhaps he suffered from the old trappers' complaint, rheumatism, caused by wading in cold streams. Still, he hoped to cross the mountains once more. With two companions he set off for Montana. But he never arrived.

Jean Baptiste Charbonneau died on May 16, 1866, at a stagecoach stop in the rural hamlet of Danner, Oregon. He was reported to have contracted Rocky Mountain fever, although other accounts identified the cause of death as pneumonia. His body was buried in Danner. It is appropriate that Baptiste died on the trail, like the adventurer he was.

On July 7, 1866, the Auburn newspaper, the *Placer Herald*, published an article entitled "Death of a California Pioneer." While the report contained some inaccuracies (the writer was clearly unaware that Baptiste was Sacagawea's son), it gives a good summary of Baptiste's accomplishments:

> We are informed by Mr. Dan Perkins, that he has received a letter announcing the death of J. B. Charbonneau, who left this country some weeks ago, with two companions, for Montana Territory. The letter is from one of the party, who says Mr. C. was taken sick with mountain fever, on the Owyee, and died after a short illness.
>
> Mr. Charbonneau was known to most of the pioneer citizens of this region of the country, being himself one of the first adventurers (into the territory now known as Placer county) upon the discovery of gold; where he has remained with little intermission

until his recent departure for the new goldfield, Montana, which, strangely enough, was the land of his birth, whither he was returning in the evening of his life, to spend the few remaining days that he felt in store for him.

Mr. Charbonneau was born in the western wilds, and grew up a hunter, trapper, and pioneer, among that class of men of which Bridger, Beckwourth, and other noted trappers of the woods were the representatives. He was born in the country of the Crow Indians—his father being a Canadian Frenchman, and his mother a half breed of the Crow tribe. He had, however, better opportunities than most of the rough spirits, who followed the calling of a trapper, as when a young man he went to Europe and spent several years, where he learned to speak, as well as write several languages. At the breaking out of the Mexican War he was on the frontiers, and upon the organization of the Mormon Battalion he was engaged as a guide and came with them to California.

Subsequently upon the discovery of gold, he, in company with Jim Beckwourth, came upon the North Fork of the American river, and for a time it is said they were mining partners. . . .

The reported discoveries of gold in Montana, and the rapid peopling of the Territory, excited the imagination of the old trapper, and he determined to return to the scenes of his youth. Though strong of purpose, the weight of years was too much for the hardships of the trip undertaken, and he now sleeps alone by the bright waters of the Owyhee.

Epilogue

As a member of the Corps of Discovery, Jean Baptiste Charbonneau lives on in history. His image as an infant in a sling on his mother's back appears on the golden dollar coin minted in 2000. He is the first baby ever to be portrayed on a circulating U.S. coin. The child also appears similarly in many statues and paintings of Sacagawea.

The owner of the property on which Baptiste's grave lies donated the land to Malheur County in the 1960s, and volunteers in the community constructed a handsome memorial to

The U.S. Mint's new golden dollar coin shows Sacagawea with the infant Pomp.

Headstone at grave of Jean Baptiste Charbonneau in Danner, Oregon —Photo by Keith Hay

Dedication ceremony for Jean Baptiste Charbonneau's gravesite, June 24, 2000 —Photo by Keith Hay

Baptiste. On March 14, 1973, the gravesite was designated a National Historic Place. Over the next few decades, however, Baptiste's grave fell into disrepair. In 2000, the Oregon chapter of the Lewis and Clark Trail Heritage Foundation restored the site, and on June 24, 2000, it was rededicated. More than three hundred people attended the ceremony, including representatives from both the Shoshoni, Sacagawea's birth tribe, and the Hidatsa, her adopted tribe. The Western Shoshoni agreed to maintain the site on behalf of all.

Historical marker at Jean Baptiste Charbonneau's gravesite —Photo by Keith Hay

Guide to Charbonneau's West

The American West of Jean Baptiste Charbonneau reaches from northern Mexico to North Dakota near the Canadian border. From east to west it extends from the Missouri River to the Pacific Ocean. A traveler today can visit many sites associated with his life.

CALIFORNIA

At Oceanside is the **San Luis Rey Mission**, built by Franciscan missionaries. Here Baptiste served as alcalde from 1847 to 1848. Restored, it is open to visitors.
(760) 757-3651. <www.sanluisrey.org>

In Auburn, Baptiste's home for nearly twenty years, is the **Gold Country Museum**, part of the Placer County Department of Museums, featuring displays about gold mining and miners.
(916) 885-9570. <www.placer.ca.gov>

COLORADO

In Platteville, on Highway 58, is **Fort Vasquez National Historical Monument**. Baptiste worked here between 1839 and 1840 or 1841. Abandoned, the fort fell into ruins, but in the 1930s it was reconstructed by WPA workers and is now a museum open to visitors.
(970) 785-2832. <www.coloradohistory.org/fort_vasquez>

Near La Junta, in southeastern Colorado, is a reconstruction of **Bent's Old Fort National Historic Monument**. Baptiste lived and worked at Bent's Fort as a hunter from 1843 to 1846. The original post was abandoned shortly after 1847, after Charles Bent had been killed by Indians and William Bent had moved away. Many years

later the fort was reconstructed, and it was made a National Historic Site in 1976.
(719) 384-2596. <www.nps.gov/beol>

IDAHO

Craters of the Moon National Monument, near Arco, is at the edge of great lava beds that spread over many acres of the Snake River plains in southeastern Idaho. Somewhere in this area Baptiste got lost in 1831 and faced a lonely trek of eleven days until he found his companions.
(208) 527-3257. <www.nps.gov/crmo>

MISSOURI

In St. Louis, on the site of the early town, is the **Jefferson National Expansion Memorial,** including the marvelous Gateway Arch and the Museum of Western Expansion. The museum's exhibits focus on the Lewis and Clark expedition but include other historical material as well. Large murals depict western landscapes that would be familiar to Baptiste and other mountain men.
(314) 655-1700. <www.nps.gov/jeff>

Baptiste spent much of his boyhood in St. Louis, supported by William Clark. The **Missouri Historical Society** has information on early St. Louis. William Clark's gravesite is also in St. Louis.
(314) 746-4599. <www.mohistory.org>

The **Lewis and Clark Center** in St. Charles has a museum and information about the expedition.
(636) 947-3199. <www.lewisandclarkcenter.org>

MONTANA

Near Billings is **Pompeys Pillar**, a great sandstone rock rising two hundred feet high out of a flat plain. The formation is a National Historic Landmark on the Lewis and Clark Trail, maintained by the National Park Service. Captain William Clark named it Pompey's Tower after Baptiste; mapmakers later changed the name to Pompeys Pillar. Clark climbed the rock and carved on it his name and the date: "Wm Clark July 25 1806". The inscription is the only remaining documented physical evidence of the expedition's presence. For information, you may call the Bureau of Land Management in Billings, (406) 896-5000. <www.mt.blm.gov/pompeys>

In Great Falls is a large **Lewis and Clark National Historic Trail Interpretive Center**, open year-round.
(406) 727-8733. <www.corpsofdiscovery.org>

NORTH DAKOTA

At Washburn is the **Lewis and Clark Interpretive Center** with various displays and programs. On the east bank of the Missouri River is a reconstruction of **Fort Mandan**, the fort built by the Corps of Discovery, where Jean Baptiste Charbonneau was born in 1805.
(701) 462-8535. <www.fortmandan.org>

Just north of Stanton is the **Knife River Indian Villages Historic Site**, which encompasses the three Mandan and Hidatsa villages where the expedition spent the winter of 1804–5. Circular depressions mark where earth lodges once stood. Baptiste and his family occupied one of these when he was a young boy.
(701) 745-3309. <www.nps.gov/knri>

In Alexander is the **Lewis and Clark Trail Museum**.
(701) 828-3595.

The **Three Tribes Museum** in New Town has artifacts and information about the Hidatsa, Mandan, and Arikara tribes. (701) 627-4477. <www.ndlewisandclark.com/sites/3tribes>

OREGON

At Astoria, **Fort Clatsop National Monument** is a Lewis and Clark interpretive site. There is a replica of the fort built by the men of the Lewis and Clark expedition for their winter home in 1805–6. While they were there, Baptiste took his first steps, cut his baby teeth, perhaps said a few words, and won the heart of Captain William Clark.
(503) 861-2471 (ext. 210). <www.nps.gov/focl>

The **Oregon Historical Society** in Portland has a museum wth Lewis and Clark artifacts.
(503) 222-1741. <www.ohs.org>

In Danner, Malheur County, is the **grave of Jean Baptiste Charbonneau**, 1805–66. It was dedicated a National Historic Place on March 14, 1973.
<www.findgrave.com/pictures/3553>

MISCELLANEOUS RESOURCES
Fur Trade
Fort Union Trading Post National Historic Site, Williston, North Dakota, (701) 572-9083. <www.nps.gov/fous>

Museum of the Fur Trade, Chadron, Nebraska, (308) 432-3843. <www.furtrade.org>

Lewis and Clark Expedition
Lewis and Clark National Historic Trail, Omaha, Nebraska, (402) 221-3471. <www.nps.gov/lecl>

Lewis and Clark in North Dakota: <www.ndlewisandclark.com>

Lewis and Clark Trail Heritage Foundation main office, Great Falls, Montana, (888) 701-3434. <www.lewisandclark.org>

National Lewis & Clark Bicentennial Council (until 2006), Portland, Oregon, (888) 999-1803. <www.lewisandclark200.org>

Oregon Historical Society, Portland, Oregon, (503) 222-1741. <www.ohs.org>

Mormon History/Mormon Batallion
Museum of Church History and Art, Salt Lake City, Utah, (801) 240-2299. <lds.org/basicbeliefs/placestovisit/1066>

Shoshoni, Hidatsa Indians
Museum of the Plains Indian, Browning, Montana, (406) 338-2230. <www.cutbankchamber.com/visit/plainsmuseum>

Three Tribes Museum (Hidatsa, Mandan, Arikara), New Town, North Dakota, (701) 627-4477. <www.ndlewisandclark.com/sites/3tribes>

Marin Museum of the American Indian, Novato, California, (415) 897-4064. <www.marinindian.com>

BIBLIOGRAPHY

Abert, James W. "The Journal of James W. Abert, from Bent's Fort to St. Louis in 1845." Ed. H. Bailey Carroll. *Panhandle Plains Historical Review* 14 (1941): 2–113.

Ambrose, Stephen E. *Undaunted Courage: Meriwether Lewis, Thomas Jefferson, and the Opening of the American West.* New York: Simon & Schuster, 1997.

Anderson, Irving. "A Charbonneau Family Portrait." *American West* 17 (March-April 1980): 4–13, 58–64.

_____. "Letter to the Editor." *Oregon Historical Quarterly* 72 (March 1971): 78–79.

Anderson, William Marshall. *Rocky Mountain Journals.* Ed. Dale L. Morgan and Eleanor Towles Harris. Lincoln: University of Nebraska Press, 1987.

Angel, Myron, ed. *History of Placer County, California.* Oakland, Calif.: Thompson & West, 1822.

Audubon, John James. *Audubon in the West.* Comp. and ed. John Francis McDermott. Norman: University of Oklahoma Press, 1965.

Bent's Old Fort. Denver: State Historical Society of Colorado, 1979.

Boggs, William M. "The W. M. Boggs Manuscript about Bent's Fort, Kit Carson, the Far West and Life among the Indians." Ed. LeRoy Hafen. *Colorado Magazine* 7 (1930): 61–63.

Brackenridge, Henry M. "Journal of a Voyage Up the River Missouri." In *Early Western Travels, 1748–1846.* Vol. 6. Ed. Reuben Gold Thwaites. Cleveland: Arthur H. Clark, 1904–07.

Carson, Christopher. *Kit Carson's Autobiography.* Ed. Milo M. Quaife. Lincoln: University of Nebraska Press, 1966.

Catlin, George. *Letters and Notes on the Manners, Customs, and Condition of the North American Indians.* 1841. Reprint, North Dighton, Mass.: JG Press, 1995.

Clark, William. "Abstract of Expenditures as Superintendent of Indian Affairs, 1823." In *American State Papers.* Washington, D.C.: Gales & Seaton, 1832–61. Microfilm.

Cleary, Rita. "Charbonneau Reconsidered." *We Proceeded On* 26 (Feb. 2000): 18–23.

Cooke, Philip St. George. *The Conquest of New Mexico and California, an Historical and Personal Narrative.* 1878. Reprint, Albuquerque: Horn & Wallace, 1964.

––––––. "Journal of the March of the Mormon Battalion, 1846–1847." In *Exploring Southwestern Trails.* Ed. Ralph P. Bieber. Southwest Historical Series. Vol. 7. Glendale, Calif.: Arthur H. Clark, 1938.

Drury, Clifford M. *First White Women over the Rockies.* Glendale, Calif.: Arthur H. Clark, 1963–66.

Emory, William H. "Notes of a Military Reconnaissance from Fort Leavenworth, in Missouri, to San Diego in California." In *The United States Conquest of California.* New York: Arno Press, 1976.

Engelhardt, Zephyrin. *San Luis Rey Mission.* San Francisco: James H. Barry, 1921.

Ferris, Warren Angus. *Life in the Rocky Mountains, 1830–1835.* Salt Lake City: Rocky Mountain Book Shop, 1940.

Frémont, John Charles, *Narratives of Exploration and Adventure.* New York: Longmans, 1856.

Gass, Patrick. *The Journals of Patrick Gass, Member of the Lewis and Clark Expedition.* Ed. Carol Lynn MacGregor. Missoula, Mont.: Mountain Press, 1997.

Golder, Frank A., and others. *The March of the Mormon Battalion from Council Bluffs to California. Taken from the Journal of Henry Standage.* New York: Century, 1928.

Gowans, Fred M. *Rocky Mountain Rendezvous: A History of the Fur Trade Rendezvous, 1825–1840.* Layton, Utah: Gibbs M. Smith, 1985.

Hafen, Ann. "Jean Baptiste Charbonneau." In *The Mountain Men and the Fur Trade of the Far West*. Vol. 1. Ed. LeRoy Hafen. Glendale, Calif.: Arthur H. Clark, 1925.

History of Sacramento County. Oakland, Calif.: Thompson & West, 1880.

Jackson, Donald Dean. *Thomas Jefferson and the Stony Mountains.* Urbana: University of Illinois Press, 1981.

———, ed. *Letters of the Lewis and Clark Expedition, with Related Documents, 1783–1854.* Urbana: University of Illinois Press, 1962.

Kennerly, Clark, with Elizabeth Russell. *Persimmon Hill: A Narrative of Old St. Louis and the Far West.* Norman: University of Oklahoma Press, 1949.

Kennerly, William. "Early Days in St. Louis from the Memoirs of an Old Citizen." *Missouri Historical Society Collections* 3 (1911): 407–22.

Lange, Robert E. "Poor Charbonneau!" *We Proceeded On* 6 (May 1980): 14–16.

Lanza, Ruth Willett. "Gentleman Mountain Man . . . Pierre Louis Vasquez." *Wild West*, April 1999, 48–54.

Lavender, David. *Bent's Fort.* New York: Doubleday, 1954.

Lewis and Clark Trail Heritage Foundation. "St. Louis in 1804." *We Proceeded On* 20 (Feb. 1994): 11–16

Lewis, Meriwether, and William Clark. *The Journals of the Lewis and Clark Expedition.* Ed. Gary Moulton. Lincoln: University of Nebraska Press, 1986–95.

Luttig, John. *Journal of a Fur-Trading Expedition on the Upper Missouri, 1812–1813.* Ed. Stella M. Drumm. St. Louis: Missouri Historical Society, 1920.

Magoffin, Susan. *Down the Santa Fe Trail and into Mexico.* Ed. Stella M. Drumm. Reprint, Lincoln: University of Nebraska Press, 1982.

Marryat, Frank. *Mountains and Molehills: Or, Recollections of a Burnt Journal.* Stanford, Calif.: Stanford University Press, 1952.

Maximilian, Prince of Wied-Neuwied. "Travels in the Interior of North America." In *Early Western Travels*. Vol. 23. Ed. Reuben Gold Thwaites. Cleveland: Arthur H. Clark, 1906.

Moore, Bob. "Pompey's Baptism." *We Proceeded On* 26 (Feb. 2000): 10–17.

"New Material Concerning the Lewis and Clark Expedition." *Century Magazine* 68 (Oct. 1904): 872–76.

Parkman, Francis. *The Oregon Trail*. Garden City, N.J.: Doubleday, 1946.

Paul Wilhelm, Duke of Würrtemberg. *Early Sacramento: Glimpses of John Augustus Sutter, the Hok Farm and Neighboring Indian Tribes*. Trans. Louis Butscher. Ed. John A. Hussey. Sacramento: Sacramento Book Collectors Club, 1973.

_____. *Travels in North America, 1822–1824*. Trans. W. Robert Nitske. Ed. Savoie Lottinville. Norman: University of Oklahoma Press, 1973.

Porter, Mae R., and Odessa Davenport. *Scotsman in Buckskin*. New York: Hastings, 1963.

Sage, Rufus B. *Rufus B. Sage: His Letters and Papers*. Ed. LeRoy and Ann Hafen. Glendale, Calif.: Arthur H. Clark, 1956.

San Luis Rey Mission. Records. Santa Barbara Mission Archives, Santa Barbara, California.

Smith, E. Willard. "Journal." In *To the Rockies and Oregon, 1839–1842*. Ed. LeRoy and Ann Hafen. The Far West and Rockies Series. Vol. 3. Glendale, Calif.: Arthur H. Clark, 1955.

Thwaites, Reuben Gold, ed. *Original Journals of the Lewis and Clark Expedition, 1804–1806*. 1904–5. Reprint, New York: Arno Press, 1969.

Troccoli, Joan Carpenter. *Alfred Jacob Miller: Watercolors of the American West from the Collections of the Gilcrease Museum, Tulsa, Oklahoma*. Tulsa: Thomas Gilcrease Museum Association, 1990.

Tyler, Daniel. *A Concise History of the Mormon Battalion in the Mexican War, 1846–1848*. Chicago: Rio Grande Press, 1964.

von Sachsen Altenburg, Hans, and Robert L. Dyer. *Duke Paul of Wuerttemberg on the Missouri Frontier: 1823, 1830 and 1851.* Booneville, Mo.: Pekitanoui Publications, 1998.

Wilson, Elinor. *Jim Beckwourth: Black Mountain Man and War Chief of the Crows.* Norman: University of Oklahoma Press, 1972.

Work, John. *The Snake Country Expedition of 1830–1831: John Work's Field Journal.* Ed. Francis D. Haines Jr. Norman: University of Oklahoma Press, 1971.

Wyeth, Nathaniel J. "The Correspondence and Journals of Nathaniel J. Wyeth, 1831–1836." In *Sources of the History of Oregon.* Vol. 1. Ed. Frederick George Young. Eugene, Ore.: University Press, 1899.

Young, Otis E. *The West of Philip St. George Cooke, 1809–1895.* Glendale, Calif.: Arthur H. Clark, 1955.

INDEX

Colorado River, 90
Cooke, Col. Philip St. George, 86–87, 89–93
Corps of Discovery, 1, 4, 5–13, 23, 47, 52, 105
Colter, John, 15, 47–48
Council Bluffs (Iowa), 42
Crow Indians, 58
Crunelle, Leonard, 2
Curtis, Cyrus, 31
Curtis and Woods trading post, 31, 33, 68

Danner (Oregon), 103
DeSmet, Father Pierre Jean, 70
Doniphan, Col., 80
Drips, Andrew, 39, 51
Duchern, Henry, 52
Duke Paul, of Württemberg. *See* Wilhelm, Paul

Emory, Lt. W. H., 85
engagés, 43

Ferris, Warren Angus, 39, 41, 43, 49, 52, 53
First Dragoons, 79
First Missouri Volunteers, 80
Fitzpatrick, Thomas, 57, 84, 88
Flathead Indians, 52
Fontenelle, Lucien, 39, 42, 51
Fort Leavenworth, 80
Fort Mandan, 7
Fort Manuel, 24, 26
Fort St. Vrain, 65
Fort Vasquez, 63
forts. *See* trading posts
free trappers, 53
Frémont, John C., 57–58, 65–69, 77–78
fur trade, 6, 18, 75, 78. *See also* American Fur Company; Hudson Bay Company; rendezvous; Rocky Mountain Fur Company

fur traders, 7, 54–55
fur trappers, 5, 15, 18, 39–49, 51–61. *See also* American Fur Company; engagés; free trappers; Hudson Bay Company; rendezvous; Rocky Mountain Fur Company

Gass, Patrick, 28
Germany, 33–36
Gila River, 90
gold mining, 99–104
Great Salt Lake, 54
greenhorn trappers, 39, 48
Guerrier, Bill, 77
guides, 31–32, 84–85
Guillet, Father Urbain, 23

"half-breed," 29, 77, 99
Hancock, Julia, 24
Hidatsa Indians, 1, 6, 7, 8, 16–19, 21, 68–69, 107; lodges of, 16–17. *See also* Mandan
Horn Chief, 51
horses, 9, 12, 54
Hudson Bay Company, 47, 51
hunting, 18, 64

Independence Rock, 42
Indian Department (Service), 27, 68
Indians. *See under individual tribes*
interpreters, 1, 8, 27, 31–32, 68, 77

Jefferson, President Thomas, 6, 16
Jefferson River, 52
Judith River, 24

Kansa Indians, 33
Kansas River, 31
Kearny, Steven Watts, 57, 79–80, 79–84, 88
Kennerly, William Clark, 70, 72, 101

Portrait of Marion Tinling at her granddaughter's wedding in Maui, painted by her daughter, Nora Hughes

ABOUT THE AUTHOR

Marion Tinling grew up in White Plains, New York, and was educated in upstate New York and Los Angeles. She graduated college in 1929, the year of the great stock market crash. That year she took a "temporary" job as a research assistant at the Huntington Library, and "by sheer doggedness I managed to stay there nineteen years."

During the Depression, Marion married Willis Tinling and had a son and two daughters. The couple divorced and she became the sole supporter of her children, working various jobs in addition to the one at the Huntington. After leaving the library, she took a position transcribing historical manuscripts for the National Archives in Washington, D.C.

Ms. Tinling retired in 1979 and moved back to California, only to begin a new career as a freelance writer. She has authored numerous articles and several books, specializing in women's history. *Sacagawea's Son* is her first book for young adults. Now the grandmother of seven, she lives in Sacramento.

We encourage you to patronize your local bookstore. Most stores will order any title they do not stock. You may also order directly from Mountain Press, using the order form provided below or by calling our toll-free, 24-hour number and using your VISA, MasterCard, Discover or American Express.

Young Adult and Children's titles of interest:

YOUNG ADULT

_____Sacagawea's Son: The Life of Jean Baptiste Charbonneau	paper/$10.00
_____The Bloody Bozeman: The Perilous Trail to Montana's Gold	paper/$16.00
_____Chief Joseph and the Nez Perce: A Photographic History	paper/$15.00
_____Crazy Horse: A Photographic Biography	paper/$20.00
_____Lewis and Clark: A Photographic Journey	paper/$18.00
_____Smoky: The Cowhorse	paper/$16.00
_____Stories of Young Pioneers: In Their Own Words	paper/$14.00

CHILDREN

_____A Field Guide to Nearby Nature	paper/$15.00
_____Beachcombing the Atlantic Coast	paper/$15.00
_____Owls: Whoo Are They?	paper/$12.00
_____Spotted Bear: A Rocky Mountain Folktale	cloth/$15.00
_____Tales of Two Canines: The Adventures of a Wolf and a Dog	paper/$10.00
_____Young Cowboy	cloth/$15.00

Please include $3.00 per order to cover shipping and handling.

Send the books marked above. I enclose $_____

Name _____

Address _____

City/State/Zip _____

☐ Payment enclosed (check or money order in U.S. funds)

Bill my: ☐ VISA ☐ MasterCard ☐ Discover ☐ American Express

Card No. _____

Expiration Date: _____

Signature _____

MOUNTAIN PRESS PUBLISHING COMPANY
P. O. Box 2399 • Missoula, MT 59806 • Fax 406-728-1635
Order Toll Free 1-800-234-5308 • *Have your Visa or MasterCard ready*
e-mail: mtnpress@montana.com • website: www.mountainpresspublish.com

A free catalog listing all Mountain Press titles is available
by calling 1-800-234-5308.